TEACHING TECHNIQUES IN ENGLISH AS A S
Series Editors: Russell N. Campbell and Wi

TECHNIQUES AND PRINCIPLES IN LANGUAGE TEACHING

Diane Larsen-Freeman

· OXFORD UNIVERSITY PRESS ·

Oxford University Press

200 Madison Avenue, New York, N.Y. 10016 USA
Walton Street, Oxford OX2 6DP England

OXFORD is a trademark of Oxford University Press.

Library of Congress Cataloging-in-Publication Data
Larsen-Freeman, Diane.
Techniques and principles in language teaching.
(Teaching techniques in English as a second language)
Includes bibliographies and index.
1. English language–Study and teaching–Foreign
speakers. I. Title. II. Series.
PE1128.A2L35 1986 428'.007 85-18872
ISBN 0-19-434133-X

Printing (last digit): 9 8 7 6

Printed in Hong Kong

To Gavin

It has been apparent for some time that too little attention has been given to the needs of practicing and student teachers of English as a Second Language.* Although numerous inservice and preservice teacher-training programs are offered throughout the world, these often suffer from lack of appropriate instructional materials. Seldom are books written that present practical information that relates directly to daily classroom instruction. What teachers want are useful ideas, suggestions, explanations, demonstrations, and examples of teaching strategies that have been supported by leaders in the field of modern language teaching—strategies that are consistent with established theoretical principles and that others in our profession have found to be expedient, practical, and relevant to real-life circumstances in which most teachers work.

It was in recognition of this need that we began our search for scholars who distinguished themselves as language teaching methodologists, especially those who had been successful in communicating the characteristics of language teaching and testing that have been found appropriate for students from elementary school through college and adult education programs. We also sought in those same scholars evidence of an awareness and understanding of current theories of language learning, together with the ability to translate the essence of a theory into practical applications for the classroom.

Our search has been successful. For this volume, as well as for others in this series, we have chosen a colleague who is extraordinarily competent and exceedingly willing to share with practicing teachers, as well as those just entering the field, the considerable knowledge that she has gained from the abundance of both practical classroom experience and empirical research in which she has been engaged over the past several years.

In a most illuminating and imaginative manner, Professor Diane Larsen-Freeman's book provides an overview and elucidation of those language teaching methods that have achieved international prominence. Each of the chapters of this book is devoted to the explication of a particular methodology, thus providing the reader with the means for inspecting and considering a number of alternative approaches to language teaching as they relate to his own teaching responsibilities. With this volume then, a critical need in the language teaching field has been met.

We are extremely pleased to join with the authors in this series and with Oxford University Press in making these books available to our fellow teachers. We are confident that the books will enable language teachers around the world to increase their effectiveness while at the same time making their task an easier and more enjoyable one.

Russell N. Campbell
William E. Rutherford

*In this volume, and in others in the series, we have chosen to use *English as a Second Language (ESL)* to refer to English teaching in countries where English is the first language, and therefore taught as a second language, *as well as* situations where it is taught as a foreign language (EFL).

· ACKNOWLEDGEMENTS ·

This book would not have been written if it hadn't been for the education I have received while teaching at the School for International Training. Indeed, much of it is based on my experience in teaching the methods course at S.I.T. I am therefore indebted to all my former and present colleagues and students in the MAT Program who have contributed to my education, and especially to Donald Freeman, Pat Moran, Bonnie Mennell, and Jack Millett, who have read earlier portions of the manuscript and whose comments have contributed directly to this book. Pat Moran should also be given credit for helping me in framing the ten questions I pose in each chapter.

Jennybelle Rardin and Pat Tirone of Counseling-Learning Institutes furnished me with many comments which helped me to improve the chapter on Community Language Learning a great deal. I am very grateful to Caleb Gattegno of Educational Solutions, Inc., for his review of and comments on the Silent Way chapter. I am also obliged to James J. Asher of San Jose State University and Lynn Dhority of the University of Massachusetts at Boston for their observations on the Total Physical Response and Suggestopedia chapters, respectively.

It has been a pleasure working with such professionals as Marilyn Rosenthal, Susan Kulick, Debbie Sistino, Catherine Clements, and Susan Lanzano of Oxford University Press. Susan Lanzano, in particular, has been a real guiding force.

For the initial faith they showed and for their continued encouragement and helpful suggestions, I acknowledge with gratitude the editors of this series, Russell Campbell and William Rutherford.

Joy Wallens deserves a special note of thanks for her superb preparation of the manuscript.

Finally, I must express my deep appreciation to my husband, Elliott, who has, as always, given me his support throughout.

·AUTHOR'S PREFACE·

This book presents and discusses eight well-known language-teaching methods that are in use today. Some of these methods have been around for a very long time and most of them have been cited before in one place or another where language-teaching methods have been written about. Since the term "method" is not used the same in all of these citations, it is appropriate here at the outset to call the reader's attention to the particular way the word is used in this volume.

First of all, a method[1] is seen as superordinate, comprising both "principles" and "techniques."[2] The principles involve five aspects of second- or foreign-language teaching: the teacher, the learner, the teaching process, the learning process, and the target language/ culture.[3] Taken together, the principles represent the theoretical framework of the method. The techniques are the behavioral manifestation of the principles—in other words, the classroom activities and procedures derived from an application of the principles.

[1] The term "method" is being used in this book in a way different from that in the familiar ternary distinction of approach, method, and technique to be found in Anthony (1963). His concept of method is too indeterminate for our purposes here. See Clark (1983) for a similar view.

[2] See also Richards and Rodgers (1982).

[3] The methods described in this book are applicable to both second-language and foreign-language teaching. Hence the term "target language" is used here to refer to both the second or foreign language that is being taught.

It will presently be seen that a given technique may well be associated with more than one method. If two methods share certain principles, then the techniques that are the application of these principles could well be appropriate for both methods. Even where there are no shared principles, a particular technique may be compatible with more than one method, depending on the way in which the technique is used. There is thus no necessary one-to-one correspondence between technique and method. Yet it is also true that certain techniques *are* frequently associated with a particular method. For the sake of convenience, therefore, techniques will be introduced in this book within a methodological context.

Second, the inclusion here of any method should not necessarily be taken as advocacy of that method by the author. Not all of the methods to be presented have been adequately tested,[4] though some have obviously stood the test of time. Accordingly, the teachers who use this book will need to evaluate each method in the light of their own beliefs and experience.

The third observation to be made has to do with the fashion in which the various methods are depicted. Each method is introduced in such a way as to afford the reader the opportunity to "observe" a class in which that method is being used. It must be acknowledged, however, that the class is always highly idealized. Anyone who is or has been a language teacher or language student will immediately recognize that language classes seldom go as smoothly as the ones we will see here. (In the real world students don't always catch on as quickly and teachers don't always perform so flawlessly.) Nevertheless, it is assumed that observing a class in this way will give readers a greater understanding of a particular method than if they were to simply read a description of it. Indeed, it is my hope that no matter what their assessment of a particular method, they will not have reached it without first, so to speak, getting inside that method and looking out.[5]

[4] See, for example, Scovel (1979).

[5] Larsen-Freeman (1983).

Finally, although I have made every effort toward a faithful rendering of each method depicted, there will undoubtedly be those who would not totally accept that rendition. This is understandable and probably inevitable. My description is, as it must be, my own interpretation of the contributions of others and the product of my own experience.

It is my sincere hope that this book will both inform and challenge its readers. If it does, then it will have made a contribution to the all-important realm of teacher education.

Brattleboro, Vermont   Diane Larsen-Freeman
1985

REFERENCES

Anthony, Edward M. 1963. Approach, method and technique. *English Language Teaching* 17:63–67. Reprinted in *Teaching English as a second language*, eds. Harold Allen and Russell N. Campbell. 2d ed. 1972. New York: McGraw-Hill, Inc.

Clarke, Mark A. 1983. "The scope of approach, the importance of method, and the nature of techniques." In *Georgetown University round table on language and linguistics*, edited by James E. Alatis, H. H. Stern, and Peter Strevens, 106–15. Washington, D.C.: Georgetown University Press.

Larsen-Freeman, Diane. 1983. Second language acquisition: Getting the whole picture. In *Second language acquisition studies*, eds. Kathleen M. Bailey, Michael H. Long, and Sabrina Peck. Rowley, Mass.: Newbury House Publishers, Inc.

Richards, Jack C., and Ted Rodgers. 1982. Method: Approach design, and procedure. *TESOL Quarterly* 16, 2:153–68.

Scovel, Thomas. 1979. Review of *Suggestology and outlines of suggestopedy* by Georgi Lozanov. *TESOL Quarterly* 13, 2:255–66.

·CONTENTS·

·CHAPTER ONE·
INTRODUCTION

As a language teacher you must make decisions all of the time. Some of your decisions are relatively minor ones—should homework be assigned that particular day, for instance. Other decisions have more profound implications. What should be the goal of language instruction? Which language teaching method will be the most effective in reaching it? What is the best means of evaluation to see if it has been reached? There is no single correct answer to questions like these. Each of you has to answer them for yourself. We believe, however, that a teacher informed about some of the possibilities will make better decisions. Making informed choices is, after all, what teaching is all about (Stevick 1982; Larsen-Freeman 1983a, 1983b).

One purpose of this book, therefore, is to provide information to teachers and teacher trainees about eight methods of foreign language teaching. By reading this book you will gain an understanding of the principles on which these methods are based and of the techniques associated with each method. These eight were chosen because they are all currently practiced today. It is not our purpose to convince you of the superiority of any one of them; indeed, the inclusion of a method in this book should not be construed as an endorsement of that method. What *is* being recommended is that, in the interest of becoming informed about existing choices, you investigate each method.

A second purpose for this book is to encourage you to examine your own beliefs about teaching and learning and about how you put these into practice. Even those of you with a great deal of teaching experience stand to benefit from considering the principles of these methods. Perhaps such consideration will help you to understand better why you do what you do.

We do not expect that you will abandon the way you teach now

1

in order to wholly adopt one of these methods. We do think, however, that there will be some new techniques here worthy of your attention. Although certain techniques are associated with particular methods and are derivable from particular principles, most techniques can be adapted to any teaching style and situation. It is not so much the technique itself as the way a teacher works with it that makes the difference.

Therefore do not be quick to dismiss a technique because, at first glance, it appears to be at odds with your own beliefs or to be impossible to apply to your own situation. For instance, in one of the methods we will consider, teachers frequently make use of a tape recorder to record students speaking the language they are studying. If you reject this technique as impractical because you do not have a tape recorder, you may be missing out on something valuable. You should first ask what the purpose of the tape recorder is: Is there a principle behind its use in which you believe and which you can provide in another way, say, by writing down the students' sentences on the blackboard rather than recording them? So try, then, as you read this book, to imagine how to adapt these techniques creatively to your own situation. You are limited only by your imagination.

We will learn about these eight methods by entering a classroom where a particular method is being practiced. We will observe the techniques the teacher is using and his or her behavior. In the even-numbered chapters, the teacher is female; in the odd-numbered chapters, the teacher is male. After observing a lesson we will try to infer the principles on which the teacher's behavior and techniques are based. Although we will observe only the one beginning or intermediate-level class for each method, once the principles are clear, they can be applied to any other level class in any other situation.

After we have identified the principles, we will consider the answers to ten questions. The questions are:

1. What are the goals of teachers who use the method?
2. What is the role of the teacher? What is the role of the students?
3. What are some characteristics of the teaching/learning process?
4. What is the nature of student-teacher interaction? What is the nature of student-student interaction?
5. How are the feelings of the students dealt with?

6. How is language viewed? How is culture viewed?
7. What areas of language are emphasized? What language skills are emphasized?
8. What is the role of the students' native language?
9. How is evaluation accomplished?
10. How does the teacher respond to student errors?

The answers to these questions will add to our understanding of each method and allow us to see some salient differences between and among the methods presented here.

Following these questions, techniques we observed in the lesson will be reviewed and in some cases expanded so that you can try to put them into practice if you wish.

At the end of each chapter are two types of exercises. The first type allows you to check your understanding of what you have read. This type relates to the first purpose for this book: to provide information about each method. The second type of exercise asks you to apply what you have learned. It has been designed to help you begin to make the connection between what you understand about a method and your own teaching situation. For this book to fulfill its second purpose, you will be called on to think about how all of this information can be of use to you in your teaching. It is you who have to view these methods through the filter of your own beliefs, needs, and experiences. It is you who have to make the informed choices.

EXTRA READING

Larsen-Freeman, Diane. 1983a. Informed choices: Review of *Teaching and learning languages* by Earl Stevick. *The London Times Higher Education Supplement*, March 11, 21.
———. 1983b. "Training teachers or educating a teacher." In *Georgetown University round table on languages and linguistics*, edited by James E. Alatis, H. H. Stern, and Peter Strevens, 264–74. Washington, D.C.: Georgetown University Press.
Stevick, Earl. 1982. *Teaching and learning languages*. Cambridge: Cambridge University Press.

·CHAPTER TWO·
THE GRAMMAR-TRANSLATION METHOD

INTRODUCTION

The Grammar-Translation Method is not new. It has had different names, but it has been used by language teachers for many years. At one time it was called Classical Method since it was first used in the teaching of the classical languages, Latin and Greek. Earlier in this century, this method was used for the purpose of helping students read and appreciate foreign language literature. It was also hoped that, through the study of the grammar of the target language, students would become more familiar with the grammar of their native language and that this familiarity would help them speak and write their native language better. Finally, it was thought that foreign language learning would help students grow intellectually; it was recognized that students would probably never use the target language, but the mental exercise of learning it would be beneficial anyway.

Let us try to understand the Grammar-Translation Method by observing a class where the teacher is using it. The class is a high-intermediate level English class at a university in Colombia. There are forty-two students in the class. Two-hour classes are conducted three times a week.

EXPERIENCE

As we enter the classroom, the class is in the middle of reading a passage in their textbook. The passage is an excerpt entitled "The Boys' Ambition" from Mark Twain's *Life on the Mississippi*. Each student is called on to read a few lines from the passage. After he has finished reading, he is asked to translate into Spanish the few lines he has just read. The teacher helps him with new vocabulary items. When the students have finished reading and translating the passage, the teacher asks them in Spanish if they have any questions. One girl raises her hand and says, "What is paddle wheel?" The teacher replies, "*Es una rueda de paletas.*" Then she continues in Spanish to explain how it looked and worked on the steamboats which moved up and down the Mississippi River during Mark Twain's childhood. Another student says, "No understand 'gorgeous.' " The teacher translates, "*Primoroso.*"

Since the students have no more questions, the teacher asks them to write the answers to the comprehension questions which appear at the end of the excerpt. The questions are in English, and the students are instructed to write the answers to them in English as well. They do the first one together as an example. A student reads out loud, "When did Mark Twain live?" Another student replies, "Mark Twain lived from 1835 to 1910." "Bueno," says the teacher, and the students begin working quietly by themselves.

In addition to questions that ask for information contained within the reading passage, the students answer two other types of questions. For the first type, they have to make inferences based on their understanding of the passage. For example, one question is: "Do you think the boy was ambitious? Why or why not?" The other type of question requires the students to relate the passage to their own experience. For example, one of the questions based on this excerpt asks them, "Have you ever thought about running away from home?"

After one-half hour, the teacher, speaking in Spanish, asks the students to stop and check their work. One by one each student reads a question and then reads his response. If he is correct, the teacher calls on another student to read the next question. If the student is incorrect, the teacher selects a different student to supply the correct answer, or the teacher herself gives the right answer.

Announcing the next activity, the teacher asks the students to turn the page in their text. There is a list of words there. The introduction to the exercise tells the students that these are words taken from the passage they have just read. The students see the words "ambition," "career," "wharf," "tranquil," "gorgeous," "loathe," "envy,"

Exercise 2A
These words are taken from the passage you have
just read. Some of them are review words and others
are new. Give the Spanish translation for each of
them. You may refer back to the reading passage.

ambition	gorgeous
career	loathe
wharf	envy
tranquil	humbly

Exercise 2B
These words all have antonyms in the reading
passage. Find the antonym for each:

love	ugly
noisy	proudly

and "humbly." They are told that some of these are review words and
that others are new to them. The students are instructed to give the
Spanish word for each of them. This exercise the class does together.
If no one knows the Spanish equivalent, the teacher gives it. In Part
2 of this exercise, the students are given English words like "love,"
"noisy," "ugly," and "proudly," and are directed to find the opposites
of these words in the passage.

When they have finished this exercise, the teacher reminds them
that English words that look like Spanish words are called "cognates."
The English "-ty," she says for example, often corresponds to the
Spanish endings -dad and -tad. She calls the students' attention to the
word "possibility" in the passage and tells them that this word is the
same as the Spanish *posibilidad*. The teacher asks the students to find
other examples in the excerpt. Hands go up; a boy answers, "Obscur-
ity." "Bién," says the teacher. When all of these cognates from the
passage have been identified, the students are told to turn to the next
exercise in the chapter and to answer the question, "What do these
cognates mean?" There is a long list of English words ("curiosity,"
"opportunity," "liberty," etc.), which the students translate into
Spanish.

The next section of the chapter deals with grammar. The students follow in their books as the teacher reads a description of two-word or phrasal verbs. This is a review for them as they have encountered phrasal verbs before. Nevertheless, there are some new two-word verbs in the passage that the students haven't learned yet. These are listed following the description, and the students are asked to translate them into Spanish. Then they are given the rule for use of a direct object with two-word verbs:

> If the two-word verb is separable, the direct object may come
> between the verb and its particle. However, separation is
> necessary when the direct object is a pronoun. If the verb
> is inseparable, then there is no separation of the verb and
> particle by the object. For example:
>
> John put away his book.
> *or*
> John put his book away/John put it away.
> *but not*
> John put away it.
> (because "put away" is a separable two-word verb)
>
> The teacher went over the homework.
> *but not*
> The teacher went the homework over.
> (because "go over" is an inseparable two-word verb).

After reading over the rule and the examples, the students are asked to tell which of the following two-word verbs, taken from the passage, are separable and which are inseparable. They refer to the passage for clues. If they cannot tell from the passage, they use their dictionaries or ask their teacher.

turn up	wake up	get on	take in
run away	fade out	lay up	
go away	break down	turn back	

Finally, they are asked to put one of these phrasal verbs in the blank of each of the ten sentences they are given. They do the first two together.

1. Mark Twain decided to _____ because his parents wouldn't let him get a job on the river.
2. The steamboatmen _____ and discharge freight at each port on the Mississippi River.

When the students are finished with this exercise, they read their answers aloud.

At the end of the chapter there is a list of vocabulary items that appeared in the passage. The list is divided into two parts: the first contains words, and the second, idioms like "to give someone a cold shoulder." Next to each is a Spanish word or phrase. For homework, the teacher asks the students to memorize the Spanish translation for the first twenty new words and to write a sentence in English using each word.

In the two remaining lessons this week, the students will be asked to:

1. Write out the translation of the reading passage into Spanish.
2. State the rule for the use of a direct object with two-word verbs, and apply it to other phrasal verbs.
3. Do the remaining exercises in the chapter that include practice with one set of irregular past participle forms. The students will be asked to memorize the present tense, past tense, and past participle forms of this irregular paradigm.

drink	drank	drunk
sing	sang	sung
swim	swam	swum
ring	rang	rung
begin	began	begun

4. Write a composition about an ambition they have.
5. Memorize the remaining vocabulary items and write sentences for each.
6. Take a quiz on the grammar and vocabulary of this chapter. They will be asked to translate a Spanish paragraph about steamboats into English.

THINKING ABOUT THE EXPERIENCE

This has been just a brief introduction to the Grammar-Translation Method, but it is probably true that this method is not new to many of you. You may have studied a language in this way, or you may be teaching with this method right now. Whether this is true or not, let's see what we have learned about the Grammar-Translation Method. We are able to make a number of observations about the class we attended. Our observations will be listed in the left column; from them we will try to identify the principles of the Grammar-Translation Method. The principles will be listed in the right column. We will make our observations in order, following the lesson plan of the class we observed.

Observations

1. The class is reading an excerpt from Mark Twain's *Life on the Mississippi*.

2. Students translate the passage from English to Spanish.

3. The teacher asks students in their native language if they have any questions. A student asks one and is answered in her native language.

Principles

A fundamental purpose of learning a foreign language is to be able to read its literature. Literary language is superior to spoken language. Students' study of the foreign culture is limited to its literature and fine arts.

An important goal is for students to be able to translate each language into the other. If students can translate from one language into another, they are considered successful language learners.

The ability to communicate in the target language is not a goal of foreign language instruction.

Observations	**Principles**
4. Students write out the answers to reading comprehension questions.	The primary skills to be developed are reading and writing. Little attention is given to speaking and listening, and almost none to pronunciation.
5. The teacher decides whether an answer is correct or not. If the answer is incorrect, the teacher selects a different student to supply the correct answer or the teacher herself gives the right answer.	The teacher is the authority in the classroom. It is very important that students get the correct answer.
6. Students translate new words from English into Spanish.	It is possible to find native language equivalents for all target language words.
7. Students learn that English "-ty" corresponds to -dad and -tad in Spanish.	Learning is facilitated through attention to similarities between the target language and the native language.
8. Students are given a grammar rule for the use of a direct object with two-word verbs.	It is important for students to learn about the form of the target language.
9. Students apply a rule to examples they are given.	Deductive application of an explicit grammar rule is a useful pedagogical technique.
10. Students memorize vocabulary.	Language learning provides good mental exercise.
11. The teacher asks students to state the grammar rule.	Students should be conscious of the grammatical rules of the target language.

Observations	**Principles**
12. Students memorize present tense, past tense, and past participle forms of one set of irregular verbs.	Wherever possible, verb conjugations and other grammatical paradigms should be committed to memory.

There were other activities planned for the remainder of the week, but in this book we will follow the practice of not listing an observation unless it leads to our discovering a different principle of the method.

REVIEWING THE PRINCIPLES

The principles of the Grammar-Translation Method are organized below by answering the ten questions posed in Chapter 1. Not all the questions are addressed by the Grammar-Translation Method; we will list all the questions, however, so that a comparison among the methods we will study will be easier for you to make.

1. What are the goals of teachers who use the Grammar-Translation Method?

According to the teachers who use the Grammar-Translation Method, a fundamental purpose of learning a foreign language is to be able to read literature written in the target language. To do this, students need to learn about the grammar rules and vocabulary of the target language. In addition, it is believed that studying a foreign language provides students with good mental exercise which helps develop their minds.

2. What is the role of the teacher? What is the role of the students?

The roles are very traditional. The teacher is the authority in the classroom. The students do as he says so they can learn what he knows.

3. What are some characteristics of the teaching/learning process?

Students are taught to translate from one language to another. Often what they translate are readings in the target language about some aspect of the culture of the foreign language community. Students study grammar deductively; that is, they are given the grammar rules and examples, are told to memorize them, and then are asked to apply the rules to other examples. They also learn grammatical paradigms such as verb conjugations. They memorize native language equivalents for foreign language vocabulary words.

4. What is the nature of student-teacher interaction? What is the nature of student-student interaction?

Most of the interaction in the classroom is from the teacher to the students. There is little student initiation and little student-student interaction.

5. How are the feelings of the students dealt with?

There are no principles of the method which relate to this area.

6. How is language viewed? How is culture viewed?

Literary language is considered superior to spoken language and is therefore the language students study. Culture is viewed as consisting of literature and the fine arts.

7. What areas of language are emphasized? What language skills are emphasized?

Vocabulary and grammar are emphasized. Reading and writing are the primary skills that the students work on. There is much less attention given to speaking and listening. Pronunciation receives little, if any, attention.

8. What is the role of the students' native language?

The meaning of the target language is made clear by translating it into the students' native language. The language that is used in class is mostly the students' native language.

9. How is evaluation accomplished?

Written tests in which students are asked to translate from their native language to the target language or vice versa are often used. Questions about the foreign culture or questions that ask students to apply grammar rules are also common.

10. How does the teacher respond to student errors?

Having the students get the correct answer is considered very important. If students make errors or don't know an answer, the teacher supplies them with the correct answer.

REVIEWING THE TECHNIQUES

Ask yourself if any of the answers to the above questions make sense to you. If so, you may choose to try some of the techniques of the Grammar-Translation Method from the review that follows. On the other hand, you may find that you agree very little with the answers to these questions, but that there are some useful techniques associated with the Grammar-Translation Method. Below is an expanded description of some of these techniques.

Translation of a Literary Passage

Students translate a reading passage from the target language into their native language. The reading passage then provides the focus for several classes: vocabulary and grammatical structures in the passage are studied in subsequent lessons. The passage may be excerpted from some work from the target language literature, or a teacher may write a passage carefully designed to include particular grammar rules and vocabulary. The translation may be written or spoken or both. Students should not translate idioms and the like literally, but rather in a way that shows that they understand their meaning.

Reading Comprehension Questions

Students answer questions in the target language based on their understanding of the reading passage. Often the questions are sequenced so that the first group of questions asks for information contained within the reading passage. In order to answer the second group of questions, students will have to make inferences based on their understanding of the passage. This means they will have to answer questions about the passage even though the answers are not contained in the passage itself. The third group of questions requires students to relate the passage to their own experience.

Antonyms/Synonyms

Students are given one set of words and are asked to find antonyms in the reading passage. A similar exercise could be done by asking students to find synonyms for a particular set of words. Or students might be asked to define a set of words based on their understanding of them as they occur in the reading passage. Other exercises that ask students to work with the vocabulary of the passage are also possible (Allen 1983).

Cognates

Students are taught to recognize cognates by learning the spelling or sound patterns that correspond between the languages. Students are also asked to memorize words that look like cognates but have meanings in the target language that are different from those in the native language. This technique, of course, would only be useful in languages that share cognates.

Deductive Application of Rule

Grammar rules are presented with examples. Exceptions to each rule are also noted. Once students understand a rule, they are asked to apply it to some different examples.

Fill-in-the-blanks

Students are given a series of sentences with words missing. They fill in the blanks with new vocabulary items or with items of a particular grammar type, such as prepositions or verbs with different tenses.

Memorization

Students are given lists of target language vocabulary words and their native language equivalents and are asked to memorize them. Students are also required to memorize grammatical rules and grammatical paradigms such as verb conjugations.

Use Words in Sentences

In order to show that students understand the meaning and use of a new vocabulary item, they make up sentences in which they use the new words.

Composition

The teacher gives the students a topic to write about in the target language. The topic is based upon some aspect of the reading passage of the lesson. Sometimes, instead of creating a composition, students are asked to prepare a precis of the reading passage.

CONCLUSION

You have now had an opportunity to examine the principles and some of the techniques of the Grammar-Translation Method. Try to make a connection between what you have understood and your own teaching situation and beliefs.

Do you believe that a fundamental reason for learning a foreign language is to be able to read the literature written in the target language? Do you think it is important to learn *about* the target language? Should culture be viewed as consisting of literature and the fine arts? Do you agree with any of the other principles underlying the Grammar-Translation Method? Which ones?

Is translation a valuable exercise? Is answering reading comprehension questions of the type described here helpful? Should grammar be presented deductively? Are these or any of the other techniques of the Grammar-Translation Method ones which will be useful to you in your own teaching? Which ones?

·ACTIVITIES·

A. Check your understanding of the Grammar-Translation Method.

1. In your own words explain the difference between learning about a language and learning to use a language.

2. Why do you think this method is one that has been derived from the teaching of the classical languages, Latin and Greek?

B. Apply what you have understood about the Grammar-Translation Method.

1. Think of a particular group of students you have recently taught or are currently teaching. Choose a reading passage from a literary work or a textbook or write one yourself. Make sure it is at a level your students can understand, yet not at a level that would be too simple for them. Try translating it yourself as a test of its difficulty. Identify the vocabulary you would choose to work on. Plan vocabulary exercises you would use to help your students associate the new words with their native language equivalents.

2. Pick a grammatical point or two contained in the same passage. Provide the explicit grammar rule that relates to each one and give some examples. Design exercises that require your students to apply the rule to some different examples.

EXTRA READING

Allen, Virginia French. 1983. *Techniques in teaching vocabulary.* Teaching Techniques in English as a Second Language, edited by Russell N. Campbell and William E. Rutherford. Oxford: Oxford University Press.

Chastain, Kenneth. 1976. *Developing second-language skills.* Second edition. Chapter 5. Chicago: Rand McNally College Publishing Company.

Coleman, A. 1929. *The teaching of modern foreign languages in the United States.* Vol. 12. American and Canadian Committees on Modern Languages.

Kelly, Louis G. 1969. *25 centuries of language teaching.* Rowley, Mass.: Newbury House.

Plotz, Karl. 1887. *Elementarbuch der Französischen Sprache.* Berlin: F. A. Herbig.

Thomas, C., ed. 1901. *Report of the committee of twelve of the modern language association of America.* Boston: D. C. Heath.

·CHAPTER THREE·
THE DIRECT METHOD

INTRODUCTION

As with the Grammar-Translation Method, the Direct Method is not new. Its principles have been applied by language teachers for many years. Most recently, it was revived as a method when the goal of instruction became learning how to use a foreign language to communicate. Since the Grammar-Translation Method was not very effective in preparing students to use the target language communicatively, the Direct Method became popular.

The Direct Method has one very basic rule: No translation is allowed. In fact, the Direct Method receives its name from the fact that meaning is to be connected *directly* with the target language, without going through the process of translating into the students' native language.

We will now try to come to an understanding of the Direct Method by observing an English teacher using it in a *scuola media* (lower-level secondary school) class in Italy. The class has thirty students who attend English class for one hour, three times a week. The class we observe is at the end of its first year of English language instruction in a *scuola media*.

EXPERIENCE

The teacher is calling the class to order as we find seats toward the back of the room. He has placed a big map of the United States in the front of the classroom. He asks the students to open their books to a certain page number. The lesson is entitled "Looking at a Map." As the students are called on one by one, they read a sentence from the reading passage at the beginning of the lesson. The teacher points to the part of the map the sentence describes after each student has read his sentence. The passage begins:

> We are looking at a map of the United States. Canada is the country to the north of the United States, and Mexico is the country to the south of the United States. Between Canada and the United States are the Great Lakes. Between Mexico and the United States is the Rio Grande River. On the East Coast is the Atlantic Ocean, and on the West Coast is the Pacific Ocean. In the East is a mountain range called the Appalachian Mountains. In the West are the Rocky Mountains.

After the students finish reading the passage, they are asked if they have any questions. A student asks what a mountain range is. The teacher turns to the blackboard and draws a series of inverted cones to illustrate a mountain range.

The student nods and says, "I understand." Another student asks what "between" means. The teacher replies, "You are sitting between Maria

Pia and Giovanni. Paolo is sitting between Gabriella and Cettina. Now do you understand the meaning of 'between'?" The student answers, "Yes, I understand."

After all of the questions have been answered, the teacher asks some of his own. "Class, are we looking at a map of Italy?"

The class replies in chorus, "No!"

The teacher reminds the class to answer in a full sentence.

"No, we aren't looking at a map of Italy," they respond.

The teacher asks, "Are we looking at a map of the United States?"

"Yes. We are looking at a map of the United States."

"Is Canada a state in the United States?"

"No. Canada isn't a state. It is a country."

"Are the Great Lakes in the North of the United States?"

"Yes. The Great Lakes are in the North."

"Is the Mississippi a river or a lake?"

"The Mississippi is a river."

"It's a river. Where is it?"

"It's in the middle of the United States."

"What color is the Mississippi River on the map?"

"It's blue."

"Point to a mountain range in the West. What mountains are they?"

"They are the Rocky Mountains."

The question and answer session continues for a few more minutes. Finally, the teacher invites the students to ask questions. Hands go up, and the teacher calls on students to pose questions one at a time, to which the class replies. After several questions have been posed, one girl asks, "Where are the Appalachian Mountains?" Before the class has a chance to respond, the teacher works with the student on the pronunciation of "Appalachian." Then he includes the rest of the class in this practice as well, expecting that they will have the same problem with this long word. After insuring that the students' pronunciation is correct, the teacher allows the class to answer the question.

Later another student asks, "What is the ocean in the West Coast?" The teacher again interrupts before the class has a chance to reply, saying, "What is the ocean in the West Coast? . . . or on the

West Coast?" The student hesitates, then says, "On the West Coast."

"Correct," says the teacher. "Now, repeat your question."

"What is the ocean on the West Coast?"

The class replies in chorus, "The ocean on the West Coast is the Pacific."

After the students have asked about ten questions, the teacher begins asking questions and making statements again. This time, however, the questions and statements are about the students in the classroom and contain one of the prepositions "on," "at," "to," "in," or "between," such as, "Antonella, is your book on your desk?" "Antonio, who is sitting between Luisa and Teresa?" "Emanuela, point to the clock." The students then make up their own questions and statements and direct them to other students.

The teacher next instructs the students to turn to an exercise in the lesson which asks them to fill in the blanks. They read a sentence out loud and supply the missing word as they are reading, for example:

The Atlantic Ocean is _____ the East Coast.

The Rio Grande is _____ Mexico and the United States.

Edoardo is looking _____ the map.

Finally, the teacher asks the students to take out their notebooks, and he gives them a dictation. The passage he dictates is one paragraph long and is about the geography of the United States.

During the remaining two classes this week, the class will:

1. Review the features of United States geography.

2. Following the teacher's directions, label blank maps with these geographical features. After this, the students will give directions to the teacher, who will complete a map on the blackboard.

3. Practice the pronunciation of "river," paying particular attention to the /I/ in the first syllable (and contrasting it with /i/) and to the pronunciation of /r/.

4. Write a paragraph about the major geographical features of the United States.

5. Discuss the proverb "Time is money." Students will talk about this in order to understand that Americans value punctuality. They will compare this attitude with their own view of time.

THINKING ABOUT THE EXPERIENCE

Let's make some observations on our experience. These will be in the column on the left. The principles of the Direct Method that can be inferred from our observations will be listed in the column on the right.

Observations	Principles
1. The students read aloud a passage about United States geography.	Reading in the target language should be taught from the beginning of language instruction; however, the reading skill will be developed through practice with speaking. Language is primarily speech. Culture consists of more than the fine arts (e.g., in this lesson we observed the students studying geography and cultural values).
2. The teacher points to a part of the map after each sentence is read.	Objects (e.g., realia or pictures) present in the immediate classroom environment should be used to help students understand the meaning.
3. The teacher uses the target language to ask the students if they have a question. The students use the target language to ask their questions.	The native language should not be used in the classroom.
4. The teacher answers the students' questions by drawing on the blackboard or giving examples.	The teacher should demonstrate, not explain or translate. It is desirable that students make a direct association between the target language and meaning.

Observations	**Principles**
5. The teacher asks questions about the map in the target language, to which the students reply in a complete sentence in the target language.	Students should learn to think in the target language as soon as possible. Vocabulary is acquired more naturally if students use it in full sentences, rather than memorizing word lists.
6. Students ask questions about the map.	The purpose of language learning is communication (therefore students need to learn how to ask questions as well as answer them).
7. The teacher works with the students on the pronunciation of "Appalachian."	Pronunciation should be worked on right from the beginning of language instruction.
8. The teacher corrects a grammar error by asking the students to make a choice.	Self-correction facilitates language learning.
9. The teacher asks questions about the students; students ask each other questions.	Lessons should contain some conversational activity—some opportunity for students to use language in real contexts. Students should be encouraged to speak as much as possible.
10. The students fill in blanks with prepositions practiced in the lesson.	Grammar should be taught inductively. There may never be an explicit grammar rule given.
11. The teacher dictates a paragraph about United States geography.	Writing is an important skill, to be developed from the beginning of language instruction.

Observations	**Principles**
12. All of the lessons of the week involve United States geography.	The syllabus is based on situations or topics, not usually on linguistic structures.
13. A proverb is used to discuss how Americans view punctuality.	Learning another language also involves learning how speakers of that language live.

REVIEWING THE PRINCIPLES

Now let us consider the principles of the Direct Method as they are arranged in answer to the ten questions posed earlier:

1. What are the goals of teachers who use the Direct Method?

Teachers who use the Direct Method intend that students learn how to communicate in the target language. In order to do this successfully, students should learn to think in the target language.

2. What is the role of the teacher? What is the role of the students?

Although the teacher directs the class activities, the student role is less passive than in the Grammar-Translation Method. The teacher and the students are more like partners in the teaching/learning process.

3. What are some characteristics of the teaching/learning process?

Teachers who use the Direct Method believe students need to associate meaning and the target language directly. In order to do this, when the teacher introduces a new target language word or phrase, he demonstrates its meaning through the use of realia, pictures, or pantomime; he never translates it into the students' native language. Students speak in the target language a great deal and communicate as if they were in real situations. In fact, the syllabus used in the Direct Method is based upon situations (for example, one unit would consist of language that people would use at a bank, another of the language that they use when going shopping) or topics (such as geography, money, or the weather). Grammar is taught inductively; that is the students are presented with examples and they figure out the rule or generalization from the examples. An explicit grammar rule may never be given. Students practice vocabulary by using new words in complete sentences.

4. What is the nature of student-teacher interaction? What is the nature of student-student interaction?

The initiation of the interaction goes both ways, from teacher to students and from student to teacher, although the latter is often teacher-directed. Students converse with one another as well.

5. How are the feelings of the students dealt with?

There are no principles of the method which relate to this area.

6. How is language viewed? How is culture viewed?

Language is primarily spoken, not written. Therefore, students study common, everyday speech in the target language. They also study culture consisting of the history of the people who speak the target language, the geography of the country or countries where the language is spoken, and information about the daily lives of the speakers of the language.

7. What areas of language are emphasized? What language skills are emphasized?

Vocabulary is emphasized over grammar. Although work on all four skills (reading, writing, speaking, and listening) occurs from the start, oral communication is seen as basic. Thus the reading and writing exercises are based upon what the students practice orally first. Pronunciation also receives attention right from the beginning of a course.

8. What is the role of the students' native language?

The students' native language should not be used in the classroom.

9. How is evaluation accomplished?

We didn't actually see any formal evaluation in the class we observed; however, in the Direct Method, students are asked to use the language, not to demonstrate their knowledge about the language. They are asked to do so using both oral and written skills. For example, the students might be interviewed orally by the teacher or might be asked to write a paragraph about something they have studied.

10. How does the teacher respond to student errors?

   The teacher, employing various techniques, tries to get students to self-correct whenever possible.

REVIEWING THE TECHNIQUES

Are there answers to the ten questions with which you agreed? Then the following techniques may also be useful. Of course, even if you didn't agree with all the answers, there may be some techniques of the Direct Method you can adapt to your own approach to teaching. The following expanded review of techniques provides you with some details which will help you do this.

Reading Aloud

Students take turns reading sections of a passage, play, or dialog out loud. At the end of each student's turn, the teacher uses gestures, pictures, realia, examples, or other means to make the meaning of the section clear.

Question and Answer Exercise

This exercise is conducted only in the target language. Students are asked questions and answer in full sentences so that they practice with new words and grammatical structure. They have the opportunity to ask questions as well as answer them.

Getting Students to Self-correct

The teacher of this class has the students self-correct by asking them to make a choice between what they said and an alternate answer he supplied. There are, however, other ways of getting students to self-correct. For example, a teacher might simply repeat what a student has just said, using a questioning voice to signal to the student that something was wrong with it. Another possibility is for the teacher to repeat what the student said, stopping just before the error. The student knows that the next word was wrong.

Conversation Practice

The teacher asks students a number of questions in the target language, which the students have to understand to be able to answer correctly. In the class observed, the teacher asked individual students questions about themselves. The questions contained a particular grammar structure. Later, the students were able to ask each other their own questions using the same grammatical structure.

Fill-in-the-blank Exercise

This technique has already been discussed in the Grammar-Translation Method, but differs in its application in the Direct Method. All the items are in the target language; furthermore, no explicit grammar rule would be applied. The students would have induced the grammar rule they need to fill in the blanks from examples and practice with earlier parts of the lesson.

Dictation

The teacher reads the passage three times. The first time the teacher reads it at a normal speed, while the students just listen. The second time he reads the passage phrase by phrase, pausing long enough to allow students to write down what they have heard. The last time the teacher again reads at a normal speed, and students check their work.

Map Drawing

The class included one example of a technique used to give students listening comprehension practice. The students were given a map with the geographical features unnamed. Then the teacher gave the students directions such as the following, "Find the mountain range in the West. Write the words 'Rocky Mountains' across the mountain range." He gave instructions for all the geographical features of the United States so that students would have a completely labeled map if they followed his instructions correctly. The students then instructed the teacher to do the same thing with a map he had drawn on the blackboard. Each student could have a turn giving the teacher instructions for finding and labeling one geographical feature.

Paragraph Writing

The teacher in this class asked the students to write a paragraph in their own words on the major geographical features of the United States. They could have done this from memory, or they could have used the reading passage in the lesson as a model.

CONCLUSION

Now that you have considered the principles and the techniques of the Direct Method somewhat, see what you can find of use for your own teaching situation.

Do you agree that the goal of target language instruction should be to teach students how to communicate in the target language? Does it make sense to you that the students' native language should not be used to give meaning to the target language? Do you agree that the culture that is taught should be about people's daily lives in addition to the fine arts? Should students be encouraged to self-correct? Are there any other principles of the Direct Method which you believe in? Which ones?

Is dictation a worthwhile activity? Have you used question-and-answer exercises and conversation practice as described here before? If not, should you? Is paragraph writing a useful thing to ask students to do? Should grammar be presented inductively? Are there any other techniques of the Direct Method which you would consider adopting? Which ones?

·ACTIVITIES·

A. Check your understanding of the Direct Method.

1. In the previous chapter on the Grammar-Translation Method, we learned that grammar was treated deductively. In the Direct Method, grammar is treated inductively. Can you explain the difference between deductive and inductive treatments of grammar?

2. What are some of the characteristics of the Direct Method that make it so distinctive from the Grammar-Translation Method?

3. It has been said that it may be advantageous to a teacher using the Direct Method not to know his students' native language. Do you agree? Why?

B. Apply what you have understood about the Direct Method.

1. Choose a particular situation (such as at the bank, at the railroad station, or at the doctor's office) or a particular topic (such as articles of clothing, holidays, or the weather) and write a short passage or a dialog on the theme you have chosen. Now think about how you will convey its meaning to a class.

2. Select a grammar point from the passage. Plan how you will get students to practice the grammar point. What examples can you provide them with so that they can induce the rule themselves?

3. Practice writing and giving a dictation as it is described in this chapter.

EXTRA READING

Berlitz, M. D. 1887. *Méthode Berlitz*. New York: Berlitz and Company.

de Sauzé, Emile B. 1929. *The Cleveland plan for the teaching of modern languages with special reference to French*. Revised ed. Philadelphia: Winston, 1959.

Diller, Karl C. 1978. *The language teaching controversy*. Rowley, Mass.: Newbury House Publishers, Inc.

Gatenby, E. V. 1958. *A direct method English course*. 3d ed. London: Longman.

Gouin, Francois. 1880. *The art of teaching and studying languages*. Translated by Harold Swan and Victor Betts. London: Philip, 1892.

Krause, Carl A. 1916. *The direct method in modern languages*. New York: Charles Scribner.

·CHAPTER FOUR·
THE AUDIO-LINGUAL METHOD

INTRODUCTION

The Audio-Lingual Method, like the Direct Method we have just examined, has a goal very different from that of the Grammar-Translation Method. The Audio-Lingual Method was developed in the United States during World War II. At that time there was a need for people to learn foreign languages rapidly for military purposes. As we have seen, the Grammar-Translation Method did not prepare people to use the target language. While communication in the target language was the goal of the Direct Method, there were at the time exciting new ideas about language and learning emanating from the disciplines of descriptive linguistics and behavioral psychology. These ideas led to the development of the Audio-Lingual Method. Some of the principles are similar to those of the Direct Method, but many are different, having been based upon conceptions of language and learning from these two disciplines.

In order to come to an understanding of this method, let us now enter a classroom where the Audio-Lingual Method is being used. We will sit in on a beginning level English class in Mali. There are thirty-four students, thirteen to fifteen years of age. The class meets for one hour a day, five days a week.

EXPERIENCE

As we enter the classroom, the first thing we notice is that the students are attentively listening as the teacher is presenting a new dialog, a conversation between two people. The students know they will be expected to eventually memorize the dialog the teacher is introducing. All of the teacher's instructions are in English. Sometimes she uses actions to convey meaning, but not one word of the students' mother tongue is uttered. After she acts out the dialog, she says:

"All right, class. I am going to repeat the dialog now. Listen carefully, but no talking please.

"Two people are walking along a sidewalk in town. They know each other, and as they meet, they stop to talk. One of them is named Sally and the other one is named Bill. I will talk for Sally and for Bill. Listen to their conversation:

SALLY:	Good morning, Bill.
BILL:	Good morning, Sally.
SALLY:	How are you?
BILL:	Fine, thanks. And you?
SALLY:	Fine. Where are you going?
BILL:	I'm going to the post office.
SALLY:	I am too. Shall we go together?
BILL:	Sure. Let's go.

"Listen one more time. This time try to understand all that I am saying."

Now she has the whole class repeat each of the lines of the dialog after her model. They repeat each line several times before moving on to the next line. When the class comes to the line, "I'm going to the post office," they stumble a bit in their repetition. The teacher, at this point, stops the repetition and uses a backward build-up drill (expansion drill). The purpose of this drill is to break down the troublesome sentence into smaller parts. The teacher starts with the end of the sentence and has the class repeat just the last two words. Since they can do this, the teacher adds a few more words, and the class repeats this expanded phrase. Little by little the teacher builds up the phrases until the entire sentence is being repeated.

> TEACHER: Repeat after me: post office.
> CLASS: Post office.
> TEACHER: To the post office.
> CLASS: To the post office.
> TEACHER: Going to the post office.
> CLASS: Going to the post office.
> TEACHER: I'm going to the post office.
> CLASS: I'm going to the post office.

Through this step-by-step procedure, the teacher is able to give the students help in producing the troublesome line. Having worked on the line in small pieces, the students are also able to take note of where each word or phrase begins and ends in the sentence.

After the students have repeated the dialog several times, the teacher gives them a chance to adopt the role of Bill while she says Sally's lines. Before the class actually says each line, the teacher models it. In effect, the class is experiencing a repetition drill where the task is to listen carefully and attempt to mimic the teacher's model as accurately as possible.

Next the class and the teacher switch roles in order to practice a little more, the teacher saying Bill's lines and the class saying Sally's. Then the teacher divides the class in half so that each half gets to try to say on their own either Bill's or Sally's lines. The teacher stops the students from time to time when she feels they are straying too far from the model, and once again provides a model, which she has them attempt to copy. To further practice the lines of this dialog, the teacher has all the boys in the class take Bill's part and all the girls take Sally's.

She then initiates a chain drill with four of the lines from the dialog. A chain drill gives students an opportunity to say the lines individually. The teacher listens and can tell which students are struggling and will need more practice. A chain drill also lets students use the expressions in communication with someone else, even though the communication is very limited. The teacher addresses the student nearest her with, "Good morning, Jose." He, in turn, responds, "Good morning, teacher." She says, "How are you?" Jose answers, "Fine, thanks. And you?" The teacher replies, "Fine." He understands through the teacher's gestures that he is to turn to the student sitting beside him and greet her. That student, in turn, says her lines in reply to him. When she has finished, she greets the student on the other side of her. This chain continues until all of the students have a chance to ask and answer the questions. The last student directs the greeting to the teacher.

Finally, the teacher selects two students to perform the entire dialog for the rest of the class. When they are finished, two others do the same. Not everyone has a chance to say the dialog in a pair today, but perhaps they will sometime this week.

The teacher moves next to the second major phase of the lesson. She continues to drill the students with language from the dialog, but these drills require more than simple repetition. The first drill the teacher leads is a single-slot substitution drill in which the students will repeat a sentence from the dialog and replace a word or phrase in the sentence with the word or phrase the teacher gives them. This word or phrase is called the cue.

The teacher begins by reciting a line from the dialog, "I am going to the post office." Following this she shows the students a picture of a bank and says the phrase, "The bank." She pauses, then says, "I am going to the bank."

From her example the students realize that they are supposed to take the cue phrase ("the bank"), which the teacher supplies, and put it into its proper place in the sentence.

Now she gives them their first cue phrase, "The drugstore." Together the students respond, "I am going to the drugstore." The teacher smiles. "Very good!" she exclaims. The teacher cues, "The park." The students chorus, "I am going to the park."

Other cues she offers in turn are "the cafe," "the supermarket," "the bus station," "the football field," and "the library." Each cue is accompanied by a picture as before. After the students have gone through the drill sequence three times, the teacher no longer provides a spoken cue phrase. Instead she simply shows the pictures one at a time, and the students repeat the entire sentence putting the name of the place in the picture in the appropriate slot in the sentence.

A similar procedure is followed for another sentence in the dialog, "How are you?" The subject pronouns "he," "she," "they," and "you"

are used as cue words. This substitution drill is slightly more difficult for the students since they have to change the form of the verb "be" to "is," "am," or "are," depending on which subject pronoun the teacher gives them. The students are apparently familiar with the subject pronouns since the teacher is not using any pictures. Instead, after going through the drill a few times supplying oral cues, the teacher points to a boy in the class and the students understand they are to use the pronoun "he" in the sentence. They chorus, "How is he?" "Good!" says the teacher. She points to a girl and waits for the class's response, then points to other students until all the subject pronouns are substituted into the sentence.

Finally, the teacher increases the complexity of the task by leading the students in a multi-slot substitution drill. This is essentially the same type of drill as the single-slot the teacher just used. However with this drill, students must recognize what part of speech the cue word is and where it fits into the sentence. The students still listen to only one cue from the teacher. Then they must make a decision concerning where the cue word or phrase belongs in a sentence also supplied by the teacher. The teacher in this class starts off by having the students repeat the original sentence from the dialog, "I am going to the post office." Then she gives them the cue "she." The students understand and produce, "She is going to the post office." The next cue the teacher offers is "to the park." The students hesitate at first; then they respond by correctly producing, "She is going to the park." She continues in this manner, sometimes providing a subject pronoun, other times naming a location.

The substitution drills are followed by a transformation drill. This type of drill asks students to change one type of sentence into another—an affirmative sentence into a negative or an active sentence into a passive, for example. In this class, the teacher uses a substitution drill that requires the students to change a statement into a yes/no-question. The teacher offers an example, "I say, 'She is going to the post office.' You make a question by saying, 'Is she going to the post office?' "

The teacher models two more examples of this transformation, then asks, "Does everyone understand? OK, let's begin. 'They are going to the bank.' " The class replies in turn, "Are they going to the bank?" They transform approximately fifteen of these patterns, and then the teacher decides they are ready to move on to a question-and-answer drill.

The teacher holds up one of the pictures she used earlier, the picture of a football field, and asks the class, "Are you going to the football field?" She answers her own question, "Yes, I'm going to the football field." She poses the next question while holding up a picture of a park, "Are you going to the park?" And again answers herself, "Yes, I'm going to the park." She holds up a third picture, the one of a library. She poses a question to the class, "Are you going to the library?" They respond together, "Yes, I am going to the library."

"Very good," the teacher says. Through her actions and examples, the students have learned that they are to answer the questions following the pattern she has modeled. The teacher drills them with this pattern for the next few minutes. Since the students can handle it, she poses the question to selected individuals rapidly, one after another. The students are expected to respond very quickly, without pausing.

The students are able to keep up with the pace, so the teacher moves on to the next step. She again shows the class one of the pictures, a supermarket this time. She asks, "Are you going to the bus station?" She answers her own question, "No, I am going to the supermarket."

The students understand that they are required to look at the picture and listen to the question and answer negatively if the place in the question is not the same as what they see in the picture. "Are you going to the bus station?" The teacher asks while holding up a picture of a cafe. "No, I am going to the cafe," the class answers.

"Very good!" exclaims the teacher. After posing a few more questions which require negative answers, the teacher produces the picture of the post office and asks, "Are you going to the post office?" The students hesitate a moment and then chorus, "Yes, I am going to the post office."

"Good," comments the teacher. She works a little longer on this question-and-answer-drill, sometimes providing her students with situations that require a negative answer and sometimes with situations that a positive one. She calls on individuals now, smiling encouragement to each student. She holds up pictures and poses questions one right after another, but the students seem to have no trouble keeping up with her. The only time she changes the rhythm is when a student seriously mispronounces a word. When this occurs she restates the word and works briefly with the student until his pronunciation is closer to her own.

For the final few minutes of the class, the teacher returns to the dialog with which she began the lesson. She repeats it once, then has the half the class to her left do Bill's lines and the half of the class to her right do Sally's. This time there is no hesitation at all. The students move through the dialog briskly. They trade roles and do the same. The teacher smiles, "Very good. Class dismissed."

The lesson ends for the day. Both the teacher and the students have worked hard. The students have listened to and spoken only English for the period. The teacher is tired from all her action, but she is pleased for she feels the lesson went well. The students have learned the lines of the dialog and to respond without hesitation to her cues in the drill pattern.

In lessons later this week the teacher will do the following:

1. Review the dialog.

2. Expand upon the dialog by adding a few more lines, such as "I am going to the post office. I need a few stamps."

3. Drill the new lines and introduce some new vocabulary items through the new lines, for example:

"I am going to the supermarket.   I need a little butter."
". . . library.   . . . few books."
". . . drugstore.   . . . little medicine."

4. Work on the difference between mass and count nouns, contrasting "a little/a few" with mass and count nouns respectively. No grammar rule will ever be given to the students. The students will be led to figure out the rules from their work with the examples the teacher provides.

5. A contrastive analysis (the comparison of two languages, in this case, the students' native language and the target language, English) has led the teacher to expect that the students will have special trouble with the pronunciation of words such as "little," which contain /I/. The students do indeed say the word as if it contained /i/. As a result, the teacher works on the contrast between /I/ and /i/ several times during the week. She uses minimal-pair words, such as "sheep," "ship"; "leave," "live"; and "he's," "his" to get her students first to hear the difference in pronunciation between the words in each pair. Then, when she feels they are ready, she drills them in saying the two sounds— first by themselves, and later in words, phrases, and sentences.

6. Sometime towards the end of the week the teacher writes the dialog on the blackboard. She asks the students to give her the lines and writes them out as the students say the words. They copy the dialog in their notebooks. They also do some limited written work with the dialog. In one exercise the teacher has erased fifteen selected words from the expanded dialog. The students have to rewrite the dialog in their notebooks, supplying the missing words without looking at the complete dialog they copied earlier.

7. On Friday the teacher leads the class in the "supermarket alphabet game." The game starts with a student who needs a food item beginning with the letter "A." The student says, "I am going to the supermarket. I need a few apples." The next student says, "I am going to the supermarket. He needs a few apples. I need a little bread (or "a few bananas" or any other food item you could find in the supermarket beginning with the letter "B")." The third student continues, "I am going to the supermarket. He needs a few apples. She needs a little bread. I need a little cheese." The game continues with each player adding an item that begins with the next letter in the alphabet. Before adding his own item, however, each player must mention the items of the other students before him. If the student has difficulty thinking of an item, the other students or the teacher helps.

8. A presentation by the teacher on supermarkets in the United States follows the game. The teacher tries very hard to get meaning across in English. The teacher answers the students' questions about the differences between American supermarkets and Mali open-air markets. They also discuss briefly the differences between American and Mali football. The students seem very interested in the discussion. The teacher promises to continue the discussion of popular American sports the next week.

THINKING ABOUT THE EXPERIENCE

Although it is true that this was a very brief experience with the Audio-Lingual Method, let's see if we can make some observations about the behavior of the teacher and the techniques she used. From these we should be able to figure out the principles underlying the Audio-Lingual Method. We will make our observations in order, following the lesson plan of the class we observed.

Observations	Principles
1. The teacher introduces a new dialog.	Language forms do not occur by themselves; they occur most naturally within a context.

Observations	**Principles**
2. The language teacher uses only the target language in the classroom. Actions, pictures, or realia are used to give meaning otherwise.	The native language and the target language have separate linguistic systems. They should be kept apart so that the students' native language interferes as little as possible with the students' attempts to acquire the target language.
3. The language teacher introduces the dialog by modeling it two times; she introduces the drills by modeling the correct answers; at other times, she corrects mispronunciation by modeling the proper sounds in the target language.	One of the language teacher's major roles is that of a model of the target language. Teachers should provide students with a native-speaker-like model. By listening to how it is supposed to sound, students should be able to mimic the model.
4. The students repeat each line of the new dialog several times.	Language learning is a process of habit formation. The more often something is repeated, the stronger the habit and the greater the learning.
5. The students stumble over one of the lines of the dialog. The teacher uses a backward build-up drill with this line.	It is important to prevent learners from making errors. Errors lead to the formation of bad habits. When errors do occur, they should be immediately corrected by the teacher.
6. The teacher initiates a chain drill in which each student greets another.	The purpose of language learning is to learn how to use the language to communicate.

Observations

7. The teacher uses single-slot and multiple-slot substitution drills.

8. The teacher says, "Very good," when the students answer correctly.

9. The teacher uses spoken cues and picture cues.

10. The teacher conducts transformation and question-and-answer drills.

11. When the students can handle it, the teacher poses the questions to them rapidly.

12. The teacher provides the students with cues; she calls on individuals; she smiles encouragement; she holds up pictures one after another.

13. New vocabulary is introduced through lines of the dialog; vocabulary is limited.

Principles

Particular parts of speech occupy particular "slots" in sentences. In order to create new sentences, students must learn which part of speech occupies which slot.

Positive reinforcement helps the students to develop correct habits.

Students should learn to respond to both verbal and nonverbal stimuli.

Each language has a finite number of patterns. Pattern practice helps students to form habits which enable the students to use the patterns.

Students should "overlearn," i.e., learn to answer automatically without stopping to think.

The teacher should be like an orchestra leader—conducting, guiding, and controlling the students' behavior in the target language.

The major objective of language teaching should be for students to acquire the structural patterns; students will learn vocabulary afterward.

Observations	**Principles**
14. Students are given no grammar rules; grammatical points are taught through examples and drills.	The learning of a foreign language should be the same as the acquisition of the native language. We do not need to memorize rules in order to use our native language. The rules necessary to use the target language will be figured out or induced from examples.
15. The teacher does a contrastive analysis of the target language and the students' native language in order to locate the places where she anticipates her students will have trouble.	The major challenge of foreign language teaching is getting students to overcome the habits of their native language. A comparison between the native and target language will tell the teacher in what areas her students will probably experience difficulty.
16. The teacher writes the dialog on the blackboard toward the end of the week. The students do some limited written work with the dialog.	Speech is more basic to language than the written form. The "natural order"—the order children follow when learning their native language—of skill acquisition is: listening, speaking, reading, and writing.
17. The supermarket alphabet game and a discussion of American supermarkets and football are included.	Language cannot be separated from culture. Culture is not only literature and the arts, but also the everyday behavior of the people who use the target language. One of the teacher's responsibilities is to present information about that culture.

REVIEWING THE PRINCIPLES

At this point we should turn to the ten questions we have answered for each method we have considered so far.

1. What are the goals of teachers who use the Audio-Lingual Method?

Teachers want their students to be able to use the target language communicatively. In order to do this, they believe students need to overlearn the target language, to learn to use it automatically without stopping to think. Their students achieve this by forming new habits in the target language and overcoming the old habits of their native language.

2. What is the role of the teacher? What is the role of the students?

The teacher is like an orchestra leader, directing and controlling the language behavior of her students. She also is responsible for providing her students with a good model for imitation.

Students are imitators of the teacher's model or the tapes she supplies of model speakers. They follow the teacher's directions and respond as accurately and as rapidly as possible.

3. What are some characteristics of the teaching/learning process?

New vocabulary and structures are presented through dialogs. The dialogs are learned through imitation and repetition. Drills (such as repetition, backward build-up, chain, substitution, transformation, and question-and-answer) are conducted based upon the patterns present in the dialog. Students' successful responses are positively reinforced. Grammar is induced from the examples given; explicit grammar rules are not provided. Cultural information is contextualized in the dialogs or presented by the teacher. Students' reading and written work is based upon the oral work they did earlier.

4. What is the nature of student-teacher interaction? What is the nature of student-student interaction?

There is student-to-student interaction in chain drills or when students take different roles in dialogs, but this interaction is teacher-directed. Most of the interaction is between teacher and students and is initiated by the teacher.

5. How are the feelings of the students dealt with?

There are no principles of the method that relate to this area.

6. How is language viewed? How is culture viewed?

The view of language in the Audio-Lingual Method has been influenced by descriptive linguists. Every language is seen as having its own unique system. The system is comprised of several different levels: phonological, morphological, and syntactic. Each level has its own distinctive patterns.

Everyday speech is emphasized in the Audio-Lingual Method. The level of complexity of the speech is graded, however, so that beginning students are presented with only simple forms.

Culture consists of the everyday behavior and lifestyle of the target language speakers.

7. What areas of language are emphasized? What language skills are emphasized?

The structures of the language are emphasized over all the other areas. The syllabus is typically a structural one, with the structures for any particular unit included in the new dialog. Vocabulary is also contextualized within the dialog. It is, however, limited since the emphasis is placed on the acquisition of the patterns of the language.

The natural order of skills presentation is adhered to: listening, speaking, reading, and writing. The oral/aural skills receive most of the attention. Pronunciation is taught from the beginning, often by students working in language laboratories on discriminating between members of minimal pairs.

8. What is the role of the students' native language?

The habits of the students' native language are thought to interfere with the students' attempts to master the target language. Therefore, the target language is used in the classroom, not the students' native language. A contrastive analysis between the students' native language and the target language will reveal where a teacher should expect the most interference.

9. How is evaluation accomplished?

The answer to this question is not obvious because we didn't actually observe the students in this class taking a formal test. If we had, we would have seen that it was discrete-point in nature, that is, each question on the test would focus on only one point of the language at a time. Students might be asked to distinguish between words in a minimal pair, for example, or to supply an appropriate verb form in a sentence.

10. How does the teacher respond to student errors?

Student errors are to be avoided if at all possible through the teacher's awareness of where the students will have difficulty and restriction of what they are taught to say.

REVIEWING THE TECHNIQUES

If you agree with the above answers, you may wish to implement the following techniques; of course, even if you don't agree, there may be techniques described below that you are already using or can adapt to your approach.

Dialog Memorization

Dialogs or short conversations between two people are often used to begin a new lesson. Students memorize the dialog through mimicry (sometimes this is referred to as "mim-mem"); students usually take the role of one person in the dialog, and the teacher the other. After the students have learned the one person's lines, they switch roles and memorize the other person's part. Another way of practicing the two roles is for half of the class to take one role and the other half to take the other. After the dialog has been memorized, pairs of individual students might perform the dialog for the rest of the class.

In the Audio-Lingual Method, certain sentence patterns and grammar points are included within the dialog. These patterns and points are later practiced in drills based on the lines of the dialog.

Backward Build-up (Expansion) Drill

This drill is used when a long line of a dialog is giving students trouble. The teacher breaks down the line into several parts. The students repeat a part of the sentence, usually the last phrase of the line. Then, following the teacher's cue, the students expand what they are repeating part by part until they are able to repeat the entire line. The teacher begins with the part at the end of the sentence (and works backward from there) to keep the intonation of the line as natural as possible. This also directs more student attention to the end of the sentence, where new information typically occurs.

Repetition Drill

Students are asked to repeat the teacher's model as accurately and as quickly as possible. This drill is often used to teach the lines of the dialog.

Chain Drill

A chain drill gets its name from the chain of conversation that forms around the room as students, one-by-one, ask and answer questions of each other. The teacher begins the chain by greeting a particular student, or asking him a question. That student responds, then turns to the student sitting next to him. The first student greets or asks a question of the second student and the chain continues. A chain drill allows some controlled communication, even though it is limited. A chain drill also gives the teacher an opportunity to check each student's speech.

Single-slot Substitution Drill

The teacher says a line, usually from the dialog. Next, the teacher says a word or a phrase—called the cue. The students repeat the line the teacher has given them, substituting the cue into the line in its proper place. The major purpose of this drill is to give the students practice in finding and filling in the slots of a sentence.

Multiple-slot Substitution Drill

This drill is similar to the single-slot substitution drill. The difference is that the teacher gives cue phrases, one at a time, that fit into different slots in the dialog line. The students must recognize what part of speech each cue is, where it fits into the sentence, and make any other changes, such as subject-verb agreement. They then say the line, fitting the cue phrase into the line where it belongs.

Transformation Drill

The teacher gives students a certain kind of sentence, an affirmative sentence for example. Students are asked to transform this sentence into a negative sentence. Other examples of transformations to ask of students are changing a statement into a question, an active sentence into a passive one, or direct speech into reported speech.

Question-and-answer Drill

This drill gives students practice with answering questions. The students should answer the teacher's questions very quickly. Although we did not see it in our lesson here, it is also possible for the teacher to cue the students to ask questions as well. This gives students practice with the question pattern.

Use of Minimal Pairs

The teacher works with pairs of words which differ in only one sound; for example, "ship/sheep." Students are first asked to perceive the difference between the two words and later to be able to say the two words. The teacher selects the sounds to work on after she has done a contrastive analysis, a comparison between the students' native language and the language they are studying.

Complete the Dialog

Selected words are erased from a dialog students have learned. Students complete the dialog by filling in the blanks with the missing words.

Grammar Game

Games like the supermarket alphabet game described in this chapter are often used in the Audio-Lingual Method. The games are designed to get students to practice a grammar point within a context. Students are able to express themselves, although it is rather limited in this game. Notice there is also a lot of repetition in this game.

CONCLUSION

We've looked at both the techniques and the principles of the Audio-Lingual Method. Try now to make the bridge between this book and your teaching situation.

Does it make sense to you that language acquisition results from habit formation? If so, will the habits of the native language interfere with target language learning? Should the commission of errors be prevented as much as possible? Should the major focus be on the structural patterns of the target language? Which of these or the other principles of the Audio-Lingual Method are acceptable to you?

Is a dialog a useful way to introduce new material? Should it be memorized through mimicry of the teacher's model? Are structure drills valuable pedagogical activities? Is working on pronunciation through minimal-pair drills a worthwhile activity? Would you say these techniques (or any others of the Audio-Lingual Method) are ones that you can use as described? Could you adapt any of them to your own teaching approach and situation?

·ACTIVITIES·

A. Check your understanding of the Audio-Lingual Method.

1. Which of the following techniques follows from the principles of the Audio-Lingual Method, and which ones don't? Explain the reasons for your answer.

a. The teacher asks beginning English as a foreign language (EFL) students to write a composition about the system of transportation in their home countries. If they need a vocabulary word that they don't know, they are told to look in a bilingual dictionary for a translation.

b. Toward the end of the third week of the course, the teacher gives EFL students a reading passage. The teacher asks the students to read the passage and to answer certain questions based upon it. The passage contains words and structures introduced during the first three weeks of the course.

c. The teacher tells the EFL students that they must add an "s" to third person singular verbs in the present tense in English. She then gives the students a list of verbs and asks them to transform the verbs into the third person singular present tense form.

2. Some people believe that knowledge of a first and second language can be helpful to learners who are trying to learn a third language. What would an Audio-Lingual teacher say about this? Why?

B. Apply what you have understood about the Audio-Lingual Method.

1. Read the following dialog. What structure is it trying to teach?

SAM: Lou's going to go to college next fall.
BETTY: What is he going to study?

SAM: He's going to study biology. He's going to be a
          doctor.
BETTY: Where is he going to study?
SAM: He's going to study at Stanford.

Prepare a series of drills (backward build-up, repetition, chain, single-slot substitution, multiple-slot substitution, transformation, and question-and-answer) designed to give beginning level EFL students some practice with this structure. If the target language that you teach is not English, you may wish to write your own dialog first. It is not easy to prepare drills, so for some extra practice you might want to try giving yours to some other teachers.

2. Prepare your own dialog to introduce your students to the "be going to" structure, or some structure in the target language you teach.

EXTRA READING

Brooks, Nelson. 1960. *Language and language learning.* New York: Harcourt, Brace and World, Inc.

Chastain, Kenneth. 1976. Chapter 5 in *Developing second-language skills.* Chicago: Rand McNally College Publishing Company.

Finocchiaro, Mary. 1974. *English as a second language: From theory to practice.* 2d ed., 62–72, 168–72. New York: Regents Publishing Company.

Lado, Robert. 1957. *Linguistics across cultures.* Ann Arbor: University of Michigan Press.

Larsen-Freeman, Diane. 1979. Issues in the teaching of grammar. In *Teaching English as a second or foreign language*, eds. Marianne Celce-Murcia and Lois McIntosh. Rowley, Mass.: Newbury House Publishers, Inc.

Paulston, Christina Bratt. 1971. The sequencing of structural pattern drills. *TESOL Quarterly* 5:3, 197–208.

Prator, Clifford. 1965. Development of a manipulative-communication scale. In *Teaching English as a second language*, eds. Russell Campbell and Harold Allen. New York: McGraw-Hill Book Company.

Rivers, Wilga. 1968. Chapters 2–4 in *Teaching foreign-language skills.* Chicago: University of Chicago Press.

CHAPTER FIVE

THE SILENT WAY

INTRODUCTION

Although people did learn languages through the Audio-Lingual Method, and indeed it is still being widely practiced today, the idea that learning a language means forming a set of habits was seriously challenged in the early 1960s. Cognitive psychologists and transformational-generative linguists argued that language learning does not take place through mimicry; since people can create utterances they have never heard before, they therefore cannot learn a language simply by repeating what they hear spoken around them. These psychologists and linguists argued that speakers form rules, which allow them to understand and create novel utterances. Thus, language must not be considered a product of habit formation, but rather of rule formation. Accordingly, language acquisition must be a procedure whereby people use their own thinking processes, or cognition, to discover the rules of the language they are acquiring.

The emphasis on human cognition led to the name "cognitive code" being applied to a new general approach to language teaching. Rather than simply being responsive to stimuli in the environment, learners are seen to be much more actively responsible for their own learning, engaged in formulating hypotheses in order to discover the rules of the target language. Their errors are inevitable and are signs to the teacher that the students are actively testing their hypotheses. Student progress is accomplished little by little, with a lot of imperfection expected in the beginning. All four skills (reading, writing, speaking, and listening) are worked on from the beginning, and meaning is thought to be at least as important as form.

Although Caleb Gattegno's Silent Way, which we will consider in this chapter, did not emerge from the cognitive code approach, it shares certain principles with it. For example, one of the basic principles of the Silent Way is that "teaching should be subordinated to

learning." This principle is in keeping with the active role ascribed
to the learner in the cognitive code approach.

In order to explore the Silent Way, we will observe the first day
of an English class in Brazil. There are twenty-four secondary school
students in this class. The class meets for two hours a day, three days
a week.

EXPERIENCE

As we take our seats, the teacher has just finished introducing the Silent
Way in Portuguese. The teacher walks to the front of the room, takes
out a metal pointer and points to a chart hanging above the blackboard.
The chart has a black background and is covered with small rectangular
blocks arranged in rows. Each block is a different color. This is a sound-
color chart. Each rectangle represents one English sound. There is
a white horizontal line approximately halfway down the chart separating
the upper rectangles, which represent vowel sounds, from those below
the line, which represent consonant sounds.

Without saying anything, the teacher points in succession to each of the five blocks of color above the line. There is silence. The teacher repeats the pattern, pointing to the same five blocks of color. Again, no one says anything. The third time the teacher does the pointing, he says /a/ as he touches the first block. The teacher continues and taps the four other blocks of color with the pointer. As he does this, several students say /e/, /i/, /o/, /u/. The teacher repeats the pattern once again and this time the whole class says in unison: /a/, /e/, /i/, /o/, /u/. He begins with these vowels since they are the ones students will already know. (These five sounds are the simple vowels of Portuguese and every Brazilian schoolchild learns them in this order.)

The teacher points to the square that represents /e/. He puts his two palms together, then spreads them apart to indicate that he wants the students to lengthen this vowel sound. By moving his pointer, he shows that there is a smooth gliding of the tongue necessary to change this Portuguese /e/ into the English diphthong /ey/. He works with the students until he is satisfied that their pronunciation of /ey/ closely approximates the English vowel. He works in the same way with /iy/, /ow/, and /uw/.

Then the teacher hands the pointer to a girl in the front row. She comes to the front of the room and points to the white block in the top row. The class responds with /a/. One-by-one, as she points to the next three blocks, the class responds correctly with /ey/, /iy/, /ow/. But she has trouble finding the last block of color and points to a block in the third row. A few students yell, "NO!" She tries another block in the same row; her classmates yell, "NO!" again. Finally a boy from the front row says, "*À esquerda*" (Portuguese for "to the left"). As the girl moves the pointer one block to the left, the class shouts /uw/. The teacher signals for the girl to do the series again. This time she goes a bit more quickly and has no trouble finding the block for /uw/. The teacher signals to another student to replace the girl and point to the five blocks as the class responds. Then the teacher brings individuals to the front of the room, each one tapping out the sequence of the sounds as he says them. The teacher works with the students through gestures, and sometimes through instructions in Portuguese, to get them to produce the English vowel sounds as accurately as possible. He does not say the sounds himself.

Apparently satisfied that the students can produce the five sounds accurately, the teacher next points to the five blocks in a different order. A few students hesitate, but most of the students seem able to connect the colored blocks with the correct sounds. The teacher varies the sequence several times and the students respond appropriately. The teacher then points to a boy sitting in the second row. The teacher moves to the chart and points to five colored blocks. Two of the blocks are above the line and are the /ey/ and /uw/ they have already worked on. The three other blocks are below the line and are new to them. Two or three of the students yell, "*Pedro*," which is the boy's name. The other students help him as he points to the colored blocks that represent the sounds of his name: /p/, /ey/, /d/, /r/, /uw/. Two or three other students do the same. In this way, the students have learned that English has a /p/, /d/, and /r/ and the location of these sounds on the sound-color chart. The students have a little problem with the pronunciation of the /r/, so the teacher works with them before moving on.

The teacher next points to a girl and taps out eight colored boxes. In a chorus, the students say her name, "*Carolina*," and practice the girl's name as they did Pedro's. With this the students have learned the colors that represent three other sounds: /k/, /l/, /n/. The teacher follows a similar procedure with a third student whose name is Gabriela. The students know now the location of /g/ and /b/ as well. The teacher has various students tap out the sounds for the names of their three classmates.

After quite a few students have tapped out the three names, the teacher takes the pointer and introduces a new activity. He asks eight students to sit with him around a big table in the front of the room as the rest of the class gathers behind them. The teacher puts a pile of blue, green, and pink wooden blocks of varying lengths (called rods) in the middle of the table. He points to one of the blocks, then points to three squares of color on the sound-color chart. Some students attempt to say "rod." They are able to do this since they have already been introduced to these sound/color combinations. The teacher points again to the squares of color, and this time all of the students say, "Rod." The teacher then points to the block of color representing /a/. He points to his mouth and shows the students that he is raising his jaw and closing his mouth, thus showing the students how to produce a new English sound by starting with a sound they already know. The students say something approximating /ə/, which is a new sound for them. The teacher follows this by pointing first to a new block of color, then quickly in succession to four blocks of color; the students chorus, "A rod." He turns to a different chart on the wall; this one has words on it in different colors. He points to the words "a" and "rod," and the students see that each letter is in the same color as the sound the letter signifies. For instance, the "o" of "rod" is white since it signifies the sound /a/.

After pointing to "a" and "rod," the teacher sits down with the students at the table, saying nothing. Everyone is silent for a minute until one girl points to a rod and says, "A rod." The teacher hands her the pointer and she goes first to the sound-color chart to tap out the sounds, and second to the word chart to point to the words "a" and "rod." Several other students follow this pattern.

Next, the teacher points to a particular rod and taps out "a blue rod." Then he points to the word "blue" on the word chart. A boy points to the rod and says, "A blue rod." He goes to the word chart and finds the three words of this phrase there. Other students do the same. The teacher introduces the word "green" similarly, with students tapping out the pattern after he is through.

The teacher then points to a pink rod and taps out /pɪnk/ on the chart. The /ɪ/ vowel is a new one for the students. It doesn't exist in Portuguese. The teacher points to the block of color which represents /iy/ and he indicates through his gesture that the students are to shorten the glide and open their mouths a bit more to say this sound.

The first student who tries to say "a pink rod" has trouble with the pronunciation of "pink." He looks to the teacher and the teacher gestures towards the other students. One of them says "pink" and the teacher accepts her pronunciation. The first student tries again and this time the teacher accepts what he says. Another student seems to have trouble with the phrase. Using a finger to represent each word of the phrase, the teacher shows her how the phrase is segmented. Then by tapping his second finger, he indicates that her trouble is with the second word:

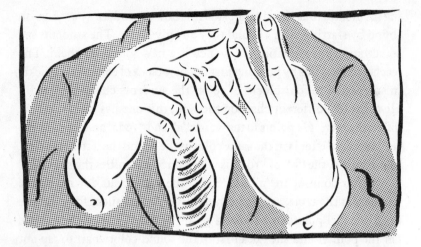

The teacher then mouths the vowel sound and with gestures shows the student that the vowel is shorter than what she is saying. She tries to shape her mouth as he does and her pronunciation does improve a little, although it still does not appear as close to the target language sounds as some of the other students are able to come. With the other students attending, he works with her a bit longer. The students practice saying and tapping out the three color words and the phrase, with the teacher listening attentively and occasionally intervening to help them to correct their pronunciation.

The teacher has another group of students take the places of the first eight at the table. The teacher turns to one of the students and says, "Take a green rod." The student doesn't respond; the teacher waits. Another student picks up a green rod and says the same sentence. Through gestures from the teacher, he understands that he should direct the command to another student. The second student performs the action and then says, "Take a blue rod," to a third student. He takes one. The other students then take turns issuing and complying with commands to take a rod of a certain color.

Next the teacher puts several blue and green rods in the center of the table. He points to the blue rod and to one of the students, who responds, "Take a blue rod." The teacher then says "and" and points to the green rod. The same student says, "and take a green rod." The teacher indicates to the student that she should say the whole sentence and she says, "Take a blue rod and take a green rod." As the girl says each word, the teacher points to one of his fingers. When she says the second "take," he gestures that she should remove the "take" from the sentence. She tries again, "Take a blue rod and a green rod," which the teacher accepts. The students now practice forming and complying with similar compound commands.

The teacher then points to the word chart and to one of the students, who taps out the sentences on the chart as the other students produce them. Later, students take turns tapping out the sentences of their choice on the word chart. Some students tap out simple commands and some students tap out compound commands.

The students return to their desks. The teacher turns to the class and asks the class in Portuguese for their reactions to the lesson. One student replies that he has learned that language learning is not difficult. Another says that he is finding it difficult; he feels that he needs more practice associating the sounds and colors. A third student adds that she felt as if she were playing a game. A fourth student says he is feeling confused.

At this point the lesson ends. During the next few classes, the students will:

1. Practice with their new sounds and learn to produce accurate intonation and stress patterns with the words and sentences.

2. Learn more English words for colors and where any new sounds are located on the sound-color chart.

3. Learn to use the following items:
Give it to me/her/him/them.
too
this/that/these/those
one/ones
the/a/an
put . . . here/there
is/are
his/her/my/your/their/our

4. Practice making sentences with many different combinations of these items.

5. Practice reading the sentences they have created on the wall charts.

6. Work with Fidel Charts, which are charts summarizing the spellings of all the different sounds in English.

7. Practice writing the sentences they have created.

THINKING ABOUT THE EXPERIENCE

Since the Silent Way may not be familiar to many of you, let us review in detail our observations and examine its principles.

Observations

1. The teacher points to five blocks of color without saying anything. The blocks of color represent the sounds of five English vowels close to the five simple vowels of Portuguese.

2. The teacher points again to the five blocks of color. When the students say nothing, the teacher points to the first block of color and says /a/. Several students say /e/, /i/, /o/, /u/ as the teacher points to the other four blocks.

3. The teacher does not model the new sounds, but rather uses gestures to show the students how to modify the Portuguese sounds.

4. Students take turns tapping out the sounds.

Principles

The teacher should start with something the students already know and build from that to the unknown. Languages share a number of features, sounds being the most basic.

Language learners are intelligent and bring with them the experience of already learning a language. The teacher should give only what help is necessary.

Language is not learned by repeating after a model. Students need to develop their own "inner criteria" for correctness—to trust and to be responsible for their own production in the target language.

Students' actions can tell the teacher whether or not they have learned.

Observations

5. One student says, "*À esquer-da*," to help another.

6. The teacher works with gestures, and sometimes instructions in the students' native language, to help the students to produce the target language sounds as accurately as possible.

7. The students learn the sounds of new blocks of color by tapping out the names of their classmates.

8. The teacher points to a rod and then to three blocks of color on the sound-color chart. The students respond, "Rod."

9. The teacher points to the words "a" and "rod" on the word chart.

10. The teacher sits down at the table and is silent. After a minute, a girl points to a rod and says, "A rod."

11. The teacher points to a particular rod and taps out "a blue rod" on the sound-color chart.

Principles

Students should learn to rely on each other and themselves.

The teacher works with the students while the students work on the language.

The teacher makes use of what students already know. The more the teacher does for the students what they can do for themselves, the less they will do for themselves.

Learning involves transferring what one knows to new contexts.

Reading is worked on from the beginning but follows from what students have learned to say.

Silence is a tool. It helps to foster autonomy, or the exercise of initiative. It also removes the teacher from the center of attention so he can listen to and work with students.

Meaning is made clear by focusing students' perceptions, not through translation.

Observations	**Principles**
12. One student tries to say "a pink rod" and has trouble. He looks to the teacher, but the teacher remains silent and looks to the other students.	Students can learn from one another. The teacher's silence encourages group cooperation.
13. The first student tries to say "a pink rod" again. This time the teacher accepts the student's correct pronunciation.	If the teacher praises (or criticizes) students, they will be less self-reliant. The teacher's actions can interfere with students' developing their own criteria.
14. Another student has trouble pronouncing part of the phrase "a pink rod." Using gestures, the teacher isolates the trouble spot for her.	Errors are important and necessary to learning. They show the teacher where things are unclear.
15. After locating the error for the student, the teacher does not supply the correct language until all self-correction options have failed.	If students are simply given answers, rather than being allowed to self-correct, they won't retain them.
16. The teacher mouths the correct sound, but does not vocalize it.	Students need to learn to listen to themselves.
17. The student's pronunciation is improved but still not as close to the target language sounds as some of the students are able to come. The teacher works with her a bit longer before the lesson proceeds.	At the beginning, the teacher needs to look for progress, not perfection. Learning takes place in time. Students learn at different rates.

Observations	**Principles**
18. The teacher listens attentively.	A teacher's silence frees the teacher to closely observe the students' behavior.
19. The teacher says, "Take the green rod," only once.	Students learn they must give the teacher their attention in order not to miss what he says. Student attention is a key to learning.
20. The students take turns issuing and complying with commands to take a rod of a certain color.	Students should receive a great deal of meaningful practice without repetition.
21. The students practice compound commands.	The elements of the language are introduced logically, expanding upon what students already know.
22. The students take turns tapping out the sentences of their choice on the word charts.	Students gain autonomy in the language by exploring it and by making choices.
23. Some students choose to tap out simple commands; others tap out more complex ones.	Language is for self-expression.
24. The teacher asks the students for their reactions to the lesson.	The teacher can gain valuable information from student feedback; for example, he can learn what to work on next. Students learn how to accept responsibility for their own learning.
25. There is no homework assigned.	Some learning takes place naturally as we sleep. Students will naturally work on the day's lesson then.

Observations	**Principles**
26. In subsequent lessons, the students will learn to use a number of different linguistic structures.	The syllabus is composed of linguistic structures.
27. The students will practice making sentences with different combinations of these structures.	The structures of the syllabus are not arranged in a linear fashion, but rather are constantly being recycled.
28. Students will practice writing the sentences they create.	The skills of speaking, reading, and writing reinforce one another.

REVIEWING THE PRINCIPLES

As you can see, the Silent Way has a great many principles. Perhaps we can come to a fuller understanding of them if we consider the answers to our ten questions.

   1. What are the goals of teachers who use the Silent Way?

   Students should be able to use the language for self-expression—to express their thoughts, perceptions, and feelings. In order to do this, they need to develop independence from the teacher, to develop their own inner criteria for correctness.

   Students become independent by relying on themselves. The teacher, therefore, should give them only what they absolutely need to promote their learning.

   2. What is the role of the teacher? What is the role of the students?

   The teacher is a technician or engineer. "Only the learner can do the learning," but the teacher, relying on what his students already know, can give what help is necessary, focus the students' perceptions, "force their awareness," and "provide exercises to insure their facility" with the language.

   The role of the students is to make use of what they know, to free themselves of any obstacles that would interfere with giving their utmost attention to the learning task, and to actively engage in exploring the language.

As Gattegno says, "The teacher works with the student; the student works on the language."

3. What are some characteristics of the teaching/learning process?

Students begin their study of the language through its basic building blocks, its sounds. These are introduced through a language-specific sound-color chart. Relying on what sounds students already know from their knowledge of their native language, teachers lead their students to associate the sounds of the target language with particular colors. Later, these same colors are used to help students learn the spellings that correspond to the sounds (through the color-coded Fidel Charts) and how to read and pronounce words properly (through the color-coded word charts).

The teacher sets up situations that focus student attention on the structures of the language. The situations provide a vehicle for students to perceive meaning. The situations sometimes call for the use of rods and sometimes do not; they typically involve only one structure at a time. With minimal spoken cues, the students are guided to produce the structure. The teacher works with them, striving for pronunciation that would be intelligible to a native speaker of the target language. The teacher uses the students' errors as evidence of where the language is unclear to students and, hence, where to work.

The students receive a great deal of practice with a given target language structure without repetition for its own sake. They gain autonomy in the language by exploring it and making choices. The teacher asks the students to describe their reactions to the lesson or what they have learned. This provides valuable information for the teacher and encourages students to take responsibility for their own learning. Some further learning takes place while they sleep.

4. What is the nature of student-teacher interaction? What is the nature of student-student interaction?

For much of the student-teacher interaction, the teacher is silent. He is still very active, however—setting up situations to "force awareness," listening attentively to students' speech, and silently working with them on their production. When the teacher does speak, it is to give clues, not to model the language.

Student-student verbal interaction is desirable (students can learn from one another) and is therefore encouraged. The teacher's silence is one way to do this.

5. How are the feelings of the students dealt with?

The teacher constantly observes the students. When their feelings interfere, the teacher tries to find ways for the students to overcome them. Also, through feedback sessions at the end of lessons, students have an opportunity to express how they feel. The teacher takes what they say into consideration and works with the students to help them overcome negative feelings which might otherwise interfere with their learning. Finally, because students are encouraged throughout each lesson to cooperate with one another, it is hoped that a relaxed, enjoyable learning environment will be created.

6. How is language viewed? How is culture viewed?

Languages of the world share a number of features. However, each language also has its own unique reality, or spirit, since it is the expression of a particular group of people. Their culture, as reflected in their own unique world view, is inseparable from their language.

7. What areas of language are emphasized? What language skills are emphasized?

Since the sounds are basic to any language, pronunciation is worked on from the beginning. It is important that students acquire the melody of the language. There is also a focus on the structures of the language, although explicit grammar rules may never be supplied. Vocabulary is somewhat restricted at first.

There is no fixed, linear, structural syllabus. Instead, the teacher starts with what the students know and builds from one structure to the next. As the learners' repertoire is expanded, previously introduced structures are continually being recycled. The syllabus develops according to learning needs.

All four skills are worked on from the beginning of the course, although there is a sequence in that students learn to read and write what they have already produced orally. The skills reinforce what students are learning.

8. What is the role of the students' native language?

Meaning is made clear by focusing the students' perceptions, not by translation. The students' native language can, however, be used to give instructions when necessary, to help a student improve his or her pronunciation, for instance. The native language is also used (at least at beginning levels of proficiency) during the feedback sessions.

More important, knowledge students already possess of their native language can be exploited by the teacher of the target language. For example, the teacher knows that many of the sounds in the students' native language will be similar, if not identical, to sounds in the target language; he assumes, then, that he can build upon this existing knowlege to introduce the new sounds in the target language.

9. How is evaluation accomplished?

Although the teacher may never give a formal test, he assesses student learning all the time. Since "teaching is subordinated to learning," the teacher must be responsive to immediate learning needs. The teacher's silence frees him to attend to his students and to be aware of these needs. The needs will be apparent to a teacher who is observant of his students' behavior. One criterion of whether or not students have learned is their ability to transfer what they have been studying to new contexts.

The teacher does not praise or criticize student behavior since this would interfere with students' developing their own inner criteria. He expects students to learn at different rates. The teacher looks for steady progress, not perfection.

10. How does the teacher respond to student errors?

Student errors are seen as a natural, indispensable part of the learning process. Errors are inevitable since the students are encouraged to explore the language. The teacher uses student errors as a basis for deciding where further work is necessary.

The teacher works with the students in getting them to self-correct. Students are not thought to learn much if the teacher merely supplies the correct language. Students need to learn to listen to themselves and to compare their own production with their developing inner criteria. If the students are unable to self-correct and peers cannot help, then the teacher would supply the correct language, but only as a last resort.

REVIEWING THE TECHNIQUES AND THE MATERIALS

Many of the ideas in this chapter may be new to you. Some of these ideas may be immediately attractive to you, whereas others may not. Give yourself time to think about all of them before you decide their value to you.

In the review that follows, the materials surveyed in this chapter (the charts and rods) have been included. While you may not have access to the actual materials discussed here, the materials may reflect ideas you can use.

Sound-Color Chart

The chart contains blocks of color, each one representing a sound in the target language. The teacher, and later the students, points to blocks of color on the chart to form syllables, words, and even sentences. Although we didn't see it in this lesson, sometimes the teacher will tap a particular block of color very hard when forming a word. In this way the teacher can introduce the stress pattern for the word. The chart allows students to produce sound combinations in the target language without doing so through repetition. The chart draws the students' attention and allows them to concentrate on the language, not on the teacher. When a particular sound contrast is new for students and they can't perceive which sound of the two they are producing, the sound-color chart can be used to give them feedback on which sound they are making.

Finally, since the sound-color chart presents all of the sounds of the target language at once, students know what they have learned and what they yet need to learn. This relates to the issue of learner autonomy.

Teacher's Silence

The teacher gives just as much help as is necessary and then is silent. Or the teacher sets up a situation, puts a language structure into circulation (for example, "Take a _____ rod"), and then is silent. Even in error correction, the teacher will only supply a verbal answer as a last resort.

Peer Correction

Students are encouraged to help another student when he or she is experiencing difficulty. It is important that any help be offered in a cooperative manner, not a competitive one. The teacher monitors the aid so that it is helpful, not interfering.

Rods

Rods can be used to provide visible actions or situations for any language structure, to introduce it, or to enable students to practice using it. The rods trigger meaning: Situations with the rods can be created in such a way that the meaning is made clear; then the language is connected to the meaning. At the beginning level, the rods can be used to teach colors and numbers. Later on they can be used for more complicated structures; for example, statements with prepositions ("The blue rod is between the green one and the yellow one") and conditionals ("If you give me a blue rod, then I'll give you two green ones"). They can be used abstractly as well; for instance, for students to make a clock when learning to tell time in the target language, or to make a floor plan of their house, which they later describe to their classmates.

The rods are therefore very versatile. They can be used as rods or more abstractly to represent other realities. They allow students to be creative and imaginative, and they allow for action to accompany language.

Self-correction Gestures

We already examined some self-correction techniques in the chapter on the Direct Method. Some of the particular gestures of the Silent Way could be added to this list. For example, in the class observed, the teacher put his palms together and then moved them outwards to signal to students the need to lengthen the particular vowel they were working on. In another instance, the teacher indicated that each of his fingers represented a word in a sentence and used this to locate the trouble spot for the student.

Word Chart

The teacher, and later the students, points to words on the wall charts in a sequence so that they can read aloud the sentences they have spoken.

The way the letters are colored (the colors from the sound-color chart are used) helps the students with their pronunciation. There are twelve English charts containing about 500 words. The charts contain the functional vocabulary of English. Although we didn't see them in this lesson, students also work with Silent Way wall pictures and books to further expand their vocabularies and facility with the language.

Fidel Charts

The teacher, and later the students, points to the color-coded Fidel Charts in order that students associate the sounds of the language with their spelling. For example, listed together and colored the same as the color block for the sound /ey/ are "ay," "ea," "ei," "eigh," etc., showing that these are all ways of spelling the /ey/ sound in English. Because of the large number of ways sounds in English can be spelled, there are eight Fidel Charts in all.

Structured Feedback

Students are invited to make observations about the day's lesson and what they have learned. The teacher accepts the students' comments in a nondefensive manner, hearing things that will help give him direction for where he should work when the class meets again. The students learn to take responsibility for their own learning by becoming aware of and controlling how they use certain learning strategies in class. The length and frequency of feedback sessions vary depending on the teacher and the class.

CONCLUSION

In this chapter we saw a beginning lesson, but the Silent Way is used with advanced students, too. For these students the same principles apply, and the same charts are used. In addition, there are pictures for topical vocabularies, books for American cultural settings, and an introduction to literature.

We have avoided referring to the Silent Way as a method since Caleb Gattegno says it is not one. Proponents of the Silent Way claim its principles are far-reaching, affecting not only education, but the way one perceives the living of life itself. Nevertheless, there clearly are implications for language teaching and you should ask yourself whether there are implications for you.

Do you believe teaching should be subordinated to learning? Does it make sense to you that learners should be encouraged to be independent of the teacher and autonomous in making their own choices? Do you think students can learn from one another? Should a teacher look for progress, not perfection? Are there any other principles of the Silent Way you believe in? Which ones?

Are there Silent Way materials which would be of use to you? Should a teacher remain silent as much as possible? Is structured feedback a useful thing for teachers to elicit from their students? Which techniques can you adapt to your own approach to language teaching?

·ACTIVITIES·

A. Check your understanding of the Silent Way.
1. There are many reasons for the teacher's silence in the Silent Way. Some of these have been stated explicitly in this chapter; others have been implied. Can you state the reasons?

2. What does the phrase, "Teaching is subordinated to learning," mean?

3. One of the mottos of the Silent Way is "The teacher works with the students; the students work on the language." What do you think this means?

B. Apply what you have understood about the Silent Way.
1. Teach some students a short target language verse which contains some unfamiliar sounds. What nonverbal gestures or cues can you develop to guide your students to produce the correct sounds, intonation, and rhythm as they learn the verse?

2. Choose a grammar structure. It is probably better at first to choose something elementary like the demonstrative adjectives ("this," "that," "these," "those" in English) or the possessive adjectives ("my," "your," "his," "her," "its," "our," "their" in English). Plan a lesson to teach the structures where:
    a. You will remain as silent and interfere as little as possible.
    b. The meaning will be clear to the students.
    c. They will receive a good deal of practice without repetition.

70

3. Think of students with a particular native language background. How will you sequence the sounds of the target language in order to teach them to these students, building on what they already know?

EXTRA READING

Gattegno, Caleb. 1972. *Teaching foreign languages in schools: The silent way.* 2d ed. New York: Educational Solutions, Inc.

———. 1976. *The common sense of teaching foreign languages.* New York: Educational Solutions, Inc.

Madsen, Harold. 1979. Innovative methodologies applicable to TESL. In *Teaching English as a second or foreign language,* eds. Marianne Celce-Murcia and Lois McIntosh. Rowley, Mass.: Newbury House Publishers, Inc.

Stevick, Earl. 1976. Chapter IX in *Memory, meaning and method.* Rowley, Mass.: Newbury House Publishers, Inc.

———. 1980. Chapters 3–6 in *Teaching languages: A way and ways.* Rowley, Mass.: Newbury House Publishers, Inc.

N.B. The materials described here and books by Gattegno may be ordered from Educational Solutions, Inc., 95 University Place, New York, New York 10003–4555, U.S.A.

·CHAPTER SIX·
SUGGESTOPEDIA

INTRODUCTION

The originator of the method we will be exploring in this chapter, Georgi Lozanov, believes as does Silent Way's Caleb Gattegno that language learning can occur at a much faster rate than what ordinarily transpires. The reason for our inefficiency, Lozanov asserts, is that we set up psychological barriers to learning: We fear that we will be unable to perform, that we will be limited in our ability to learn, that we will fail. One result is that we do not use the full mental powers that we have. According to Lozanov and others, we may be using only five to ten percent of our mental capacity. In order to make better use of our mental reserves, the limitations we think we have need to be "desuggested." Suggestopedia, the application of the study of suggestion to pedagogy, has been developed to help students eliminate the feeling that they cannot be successful and, thus, to help them overcome the barriers to learning.

Let us now see for ourselves how the principles of Suggestopedia are applied to language teaching. We will visit a university class in Egypt being taught English by this method. There are sixteen students in the class. They are beginners. The class meets for two hours, three mornings a week.

EXPERIENCE*

The first thing we notice when we enter the classroom is how different this room is compared with all the other classrooms we've been in so far. The students are seated in cushioned armchairs that are arranged

---

* The lesson described here is in part based on ones the author observed taught by Dan Dugas and Lynn Dhority, respectively.

in a semicircle facing the front of the room. The lighting is dim. There is soft music playing. There are several posters on the walls. Most of them are travel posters with scenes from America; a few, however, contain grammatical information. One has the conjugation of the verb "be" and the subject pronouns; another has the object and possessive pronouns.

The teacher greets the students in Arabic and tells them that they are about to begin a new and exciting experience in language learning. She says confidently, "You won't need to try to learn. It will just come naturally. Sit back and enjoy yourself."

The teacher puts on a record of *The Grand Canyon Suite* and invites the students to close their eyes and to become aware of their breathing. "In, out. In, out," she says almost in a whisper. She then invites the students to take an imaginary trip with her. She tells them that they are going to visit America. She will be their guide. She describes the airplane flight, what they will see when they first land

and how they will feel in the airport. She tells them to listen to the
English all around them and to feel themselves replying fluently in
English to questions posed to them by the customs and immigration
officials. "Now," she says, "slowly bring your awareness back to this
room, its sounds and its smells. When you are ready, open your eyes.
Welcome to English!"

One by one the students open their eyes. When they have all done
so, the teacher tells them that they are all about to get new names—
English ones. "It will be fun," she says. Besides, she tells them, they
will need new identities (ones they can play with) to go along with this
new experience. She shows the class a poster with different English
names printed in color in the Roman alphabet. The students are familiar
with the Roman alphabet from their earlier study of French. There
are men's names in one column and women's names in another. She
tells them that they are each to choose a name. She pronounces each
name and has the students repeat the pronunciation. One by one the
students say which name they have chosen.

Next, she tells them that during the course they will create an
imaginary biography about the life of their new identity. But for now,
she says, they should just choose a profession to go with the new name.
Using pantomime to help the students understand, the teacher acts
out various occupations, such as pilot, singer, carpenter, and artist.
The students choose what they want to be.

The teacher greets each student using his new name and asks
him a few questions in English about his new occupation. Through
her actions the students understand the meaning and they reply "yes"
or "no." She then teaches them a short English dialog in which two
people greet each other and inquire what each other does for a living.
After practicing the dialog with the group and with individual students,
the teacher tells the class to pretend that they are each at a party where
they don't know anyone. The students stand up and walk around the
room, greeting one another.

Next the teacher announces to the class that they will be beginning a new adventure. She distributes a twenty-page handout. The
handout contains a lengthy dialog entitled "To Want To Is To Be Able
To," which the teacher translates into Arabic. She has the students
turn the page. On the right page are two columns of print: In the left

one is the English dialog; in the right, the Arabic translation. On the left page are some comments in Arabic about certain of the English vocabulary items and grammatical structures the students will encounter in the dialog on the facing page.

Partly in Arabic, partly in English, and partly through pantomime, the teacher outlines the dialog's story. She also calls her students' attention to some of the comments regarding vocabulary and grammar on the left-hand pages. Then she tells them in Arabic that she is going to read the dialog to them in English and that they should follow along as she reads. She will give them sufficient time to look at both the English and the Arabic. "Just enjoy," she concludes.

The teacher puts on some music. It's Mozart's Violin Concerto no. 5. After a couple of minutes, in a quiet voice she begins to read the text. Her reading appears to be molded by the music as her intonation and volume rise and fall with the music. She speaks at a slow pace.

The teacher then explains that she will read the dialog again. This time she suggests that the students put down their scripts, close their eyes, and just listen. The second time she reads the dialog, she appears to be speaking at a normal rate. She has changed the music to Handel's *Water Music*. She makes no attempt this time to match her voice to the music. With the end of the second reading, the class is over. There is no homework assigned; however, the teacher suggests that if the students want to do something, they could read over the dialog once before they go to bed and once when they get up in the morning.

We decide to attend the next class to see how the teacher will work with the new material she has presented. After greeting the students and having them introduce themselves in their new identities once again, the teacher asks the students to take out their dialog scripts.

Next, the teacher pulls out a hat from a bag. She puts it on her head, points to herself, and names a character from the dialog. She indicates that she wants someone else to wear the hat. A girl volunteers to do so. Three more hats are taken out of the teacher's bag and, with a great deal of playfulness, they are distributed. The teacher turns to the four students wearing the hats and asks them to read a portion of the dialog, imagining that they are the character whose hat they wear. When they finish their portion of dialog, four different students get to wear the hats and continue reading the script. This group is asked to read it in a sad way. The next group of four read it in an angry way, and the last group of four in an amorous way.

The teacher then asks for four new volunteers. She tells them to pretend they are auditioning for a role in a Broadway play. They want very much to win the role. In order to impress the director of the play, they must read their lines very dramatically. The first group reads several pages of the dialog in this manner, and following groups do this as well.

Next, the teacher asks questions in English about the dialog. She also asks students to give her the English translation of an Arabic sentence and vice versa. Sometimes she asks the students to repeat an English line after her; still other times, she addresses a question from the dialog to an individual student.

Next, she teaches the students a children's alphabet song containing English names and occupations, "*A*, my name is Alice; my husband's name is Alex. We live in America, and we sell apples. *B*, my name is Barbara; my husband's name is Bert. We live in Brazil, and we sell books." The students are laughing and clapping as they sing along.

After the song, the teacher has the students stand up and get in a circle. She takes out a medium-sized soft ball. She throws the ball to one student and, while she's throwing it, she asks him what his name is in English. He catches the ball as he says, "My name is Richard." She indicates that he is to throw the ball to another student while posing a question to him. Richard asks, "What you do?" (The teacher says nothing, but we notice later that when it is the teacher's turn again, her question is "What do you do?") The student replies, "I am a conductor." The game continues on in this manner with the students posing questions to one another as they throw the ball. The second class is now over. Again, there is no homework assigned, other than to read over the dialog if a student so wishes.

During the third class of the week, the students will continue to work with this dialog. They will move away from reading it, however, and move toward using the new language in a creative way. They will play some competitive games, do role-plays (see description in the techniques review) and skits. Next week, the class will be introduced to a new dialog and the basic sequence of lessons we observed here will be repeated.

THINKING ABOUT THE EXPERIENCE

Let us now investigate Suggestopedia in our usual fashion. First, we will list our observations. From these, we will attempt to uncover the principles of Suggestopedia.

Observations	Principles
1. The classroom is unusual: The students are seated in cushioned armchairs, the lighting is dim, soft music is playing.	Learning is facilitated in a relaxed, comfortable environment.
2. Among the posters hanging around the room are several containing grammatical information.	A student can learn from what is present in the environment, even if his attention is not directed to it ("Peripheral Learning").
3. The teacher speaks reassuringly.	If the student trusts and respects the teacher's authority, he will accept and retain information better.
4. The teacher tells them that learning the target language will be easy and enjoyable.	The teacher should recognize that learners bring certain psychological barriers with them to the learning situation. She should attempt to "desuggest" these.
5. The teacher invites the students to take a mental trip with her.	Activating the learners' imagination will aid learning.

Observations	**Principles**
6. The teacher suggests that the students feel themselves replying fluently in English to the questions posed to them.	The teacher attempts to increase her students' confidence that they will be successful learners. The more confident the students feel, the better they will learn.
7. The students choose new names and identities.	Assuming a new identity enhances students' feeling of security and allows them to be more open. They feel less inhibited since their performance is really that of a different person.
8. The students greet each other and inquire about each other's occupations.	The dialog that the students learn contains language they can use immediately.
9. The students use the new English sentences as if they were at a party.	When their attention is off the form of the language, and on the process of communicating, students will learn best.
10. The teacher distributes a lengthy handout to the class. The title of the dialog is "To Want To Is To Be Able To."	The teacher should integrate indirect positive suggestions ("there is no limit to what you can do") into the learning situation.
11. The teacher briefly mentions a few points about English grammar and vocabulary.	The teacher should present and explain the grammar and vocabulary, but not dwell on them.
12. In the left column is the dialog in the target language. In the right column is the mother tongue translation.	One way that meaning is made clear is through mother tongue translation.

Observations

13. The teacher reads the dialog with a musical accompaniment. She matches her voice to the volume and intonation of the music.

14. The teacher reads the script a second time as the students close their eyes and listen. This is done to different music.

15. For homework, the students are to read the dialog at night and in the morning.

16. The teacher gives the students hats to wear for the different characters in the dialog. The students take turns reading portions of the dialog.

17. The teacher instructs the students to pretend they are auditioning for a play.

Principles

Communication takes place on "two planes": on one the linguistic message is encoded; and on the other are factors which influence the linguistic message. On the conscious plane, the learner attends to the language; on the subconscious plane, the music suggests that learning is easy and pleasant. When there is a unity between conscious and subconscious, learning is enhanced.

A pseudo-passive state, such as the state one experiences when listening to a concert, is ideal for overcoming psychological barriers and for taking advantage of learning potential.

At these times, the distinction between the conscious and the subconscious is most blurred and, therefore, optimal learning can occur.

Dramatization is a particularly valuable way of playfully activating the material. Fantasy reduces barriers to learning.

The fine arts (music, art, and drama) enable suggestions to reach the subconscious. The arts should, therefore, be integrated as much as possible into the teaching process.

Observations

18. The teacher leads the class in various activities involving the dialog, for example, question-and-answer, repetition, and translation.

19. She teaches the students a children's song.

20. The teacher and students play a question-and-answer game with a ball.

21. The student makes an error by saying, "How you do?" The teacher ignores the error at the time, but later uses the correct question structure herself.

Principles

The teacher should help the students "activate" the material to which they have been exposed. The means of doing this should be varied so as to avoid repetition as much as possible. Novelty aids acquisition.

Music and movement reinforce the linguistic material. It is desirable that students achieve a state of "infantilization"—having a childlike attitude—so that they will be more open to learning. If they trust the teacher, they will reach this state more easily.

In an atmosphere of play, the conscious attention of the learner does not focus on linguistic forms, but rather on using the language. Learning can be fun.

Errors are to be tolerated, the emphasis being on content, not form. The teacher should use the form a little later so the students will hear it used correctly.

REVIEWING THE PRINCIPLES

Let us now follow our usual procedure of reviewing the principles of a method by answering our ten questions.

1. What are the goals of teachers who use Suggestopedia?

Teachers hope to accelerate the process by which students learn to use a foreign language for everyday communication. In order to do this, more of the students' mental powers must be tapped. This is accomplished by desuggesting the psychological barriers learners bring with them to the learning situation.

2. What is the role of the teacher? What is the role of the students?

The teacher is the authority in the classroom. In order for the method to be successful, the students must trust and respect her. The students will retain information better from someone in whom they have confidence since they will be more responsive to her "desuggesting" their limitations and suggesting how easy it will be for them to succeed.

Once the students trust the teacher, they can undergo infantilization—adopting a childlike role. If they feel secure, they can be more spontaneous and less inhibited.

3. What are some characteristics of the teaching/learning process?

A Suggestopedic course is conducted in a classroom in which students are as comfortable as possible. Ideally, easy chairs, soft lighting, and music are all available to contribute to a relaxing environment. Posters displaying grammatical information about the target language are hung around the room in order to take advantage of students' peripheral learning. The posters are changed every few weeks.

Students select target language names and choose new occupations. During the course they create whole biographies to go along with their new identities.

The texts students work from are handouts containing lengthy dialogs in the target language. Next to the dialog is a translation in the students' native language. There are also some notes on the vocabulary and grammar in the dialog.

The teacher presents the dialog during two concerts. These represent the first major phase (the receptive phase). In the first concert the teacher reads the dialog, matching her voice to the rhythm and pitch of the music. In this way, the "whole brain" (both the left and the right hemispheres) of the students becomes activated. The students follow the target language dialog as the teacher reads it out loud. They also check the translation. During the second concert, the students simply relax while the teacher reads the dialog at a normal rate of speed. For homework the students read over the dialog just before they go to sleep, and again when they get up the next morning.

What follows is the second major phase (the activation phase), in which students engage in various activities designed to help them gain facility with the new material. The activities include dramatizations, games, songs, and question-and-answer exercises.

4. What is the nature of student-teacher interaction? What is the nature of student-student interaction?

The teacher initiates interactions with the whole group of students and with individuals right from the beginning of a language course. Initially, the students can only respond nonverbally or with a few target language words they have practiced. Later the students have more control of the target language and can respond more appropriately and even initiate interaction themselves. Students interact with each other from the beginning in various activities directed by the teacher.

5. How are the feelings of the students dealt with?

A great deal of attention is given to students' feelings in this method. One of the fundamental principles of the method is that if students are relaxed and confident, they will not need to try hard to learn the language. It will just come naturally and easily.

It is considered important in this method that the psychological barriers that students bring with them be desuggested. Direct and indirect positive suggestions are made to enhance students' self-confidence and to convince them that success is obtainable.

Students also choose target language names on the assumption that a new identity makes students feel more secure and thus more open to learning.

6. How is language viewed? How is culture viewed?

Language is the first of two planes in the two-plane process of communication. In the second plane are the factors which influence the linguistic message. For example, the way one dresses or the nonverbal behavior one uses affects how one's linguistic message is interpreted.

The culture which students learn concerns the everyday life of people who speak the language. The use of the fine arts is also common in Suggestopedic classes.

7. What areas of language are emphasized? What language skills are emphasized?

Vocabulary is emphasized. Claims about the success of the method often focus on the large number of words that can be acquired. Grammar is dealt with explicitly but minimally. In fact, it is believed that students will learn best if their conscious attention is focused, not on the language forms, but on using the language.

Speaking communicatively is emphasized. Students also read the target language (for example, dialogs) and write (for example, imaginative compositions).

8. What is the role of the students' native language?

Native language translation is used to make the meaning of the dialog clear. The teacher also uses the mother tongue in class when necessary. As the course proceeds, the teacher uses the native language less and less.

9. How is evaluation accomplished?

Evaluation usually is conducted on students' normal in-class performance and not through formal tests, which would threaten the relaxed atmosphere considered essential for accelerated learning.

10. How does the teacher respond to student errors?

At least at beginning levels, errors are not corrected immediately since the emphasis is on students communicating their intended meaning. When errors of form do occur, the teacher uses the form correctly later on during class.

REVIEWING THE TECHNIQUES AND THE CLASSROOM SET-UP

If you find Suggestopedia's principles meaningful, you may want to try some of the following techniques or to alter your classroom environment. Even if they don't all appeal to you, there may be some elements you could usefully adapt to your own teaching style.

Classroom Set-up

The challenge for the teacher is to create a classroom environment which does not look or feel like a normal classroom. This was accomplished in the classroom we visited by the use of dim lights, soft music, cushioned armchairs, and walls decorated with scenes from a country where the target language is spoken. These conditions are not always possible. However, the teacher should try to provide as relaxed and comfortable an environment as possible.

Peripheral Learning

This technique is based upon the idea that we perceive much more in our environment than that to which we consciously attend. It is claimed that, by putting posters containing grammatical information about the target language on the classroom walls, students will absorb the necessary facts effortlessly. The teacher may or may not call attention to the posters. They are changed from time to time to provide grammatical information that is appropriate to what the students are studying.

Positive Suggestion

It is the teacher's responsibility to orchestrate the suggestive factors in a learning situation, thereby helping students break down the barriers to learning that they bring with them. Teachers can do this through direct and indirect means. Direct suggestion appeals to the students' consciousness: A teacher tells students they are going to be successful. But indirect suggestion, which appeals to the students' subconscious, is actually the more powerful of the two. For example, indirect suggestion was accomplished in the class we visited through the use of music and a comfortable physical environment. It helped the students relax and feel that the learning experience was going to be a pleasant one.

Visualization

Visualization can be a vehicle for positive suggestion or it can be used simply to relax one's students. Students are asked to close their eyes and to concentrate on their breathing. After a minute or so, the teacher, speaking in a quiet voice, describes a scene or event. The description is detailed so students feel they are really there. When the description is complete, the teacher asks the students to slowly open their eyes and to return to the present.

Some teachers have used such visualization exercises to activate student creativity just before their students do something in the target language—writing a composition, for example.

Choose a New Identity

The students choose a target language name and a new occupation. As the course continues, the students have an opportunity to develop a whole biography about their fictional selves. For instance, later on they may be asked to talk or write about their fictional hometown, childhood, and family.

Role-play

Students are asked to pretend temporarily that they are someone else and to perform in the target language as if they were that person. They are often asked to create their own lines relevant to the situation. In the lesson we observed, the students were asked to pretend they were at a party and were going around meeting other people there.

First Concert

The two concerts are components of the receptive phase of the lesson. After the teacher has introduced the story as related in the dialog and has called his students' attention to some particular grammatical points that arise in it, he reads the dialog in the target language. The students have copies of the dialog in the target language and their mother tongue and refer to it as the teacher is reading.

Music is played. After a few minutes, the teacher begins a slow, dramatic reading, synchronized in intonation with the music. The music is classical; the early Romantic period is suggested. The teacher's voice is usually hushed, but rises and falls with the music.

Second Concert

In the second phase, the students are asked to put their scripts aside. They simply close their eyes and listen as the teacher reads the dialog at a normal rate of speed. The teacher is seated and reads with musical accompaniment. This time the content governs the way the teacher reads the script, not the music, which is pre-Classical or Baroque. At the end of this concert, the class ends for the day.

Primary Activation

This technique and the one that follows are components of the active phase of the lesson. The students playfully reread the target language dialog out loud, as individuals or in groups. In the lesson we observed, three groups of students read parts of the dialog in a particular manner: the first group, sadly; the next, angrily; the last, amorously.

Secondary Activation

The students engage in various activities designed to help them learn the new material and use it spontaneously. Activities particularly recommended for this phase include singing, dancing, dramatizations, and games. The important thing is that the activities are varied and don't allow the students to focus on the form of the linguistic message, just the communicative intent.

CONCLUSION

What connection, if any, can you make between Suggestopedia and your approach to teaching? Does it make sense to you that when your students are relaxed and comfortable, their learning will be facilitated? Should the teacher's role be one of being a respected and trusted authority? Should direct and indirect suggestions be used? Should learning be made as enjoyable as possible? Which, if any, of the other principles of Suggestopedia do you accept?

Do you think students can learn peripherally? Would it be useful for your students to develop a new target language identity? Would you consider presenting new material with a musical accompaniment? Are any of the activities of the activation phase of use to you?

·ACTIVITIES·

A. Check your understanding of Suggestopedia.

1. What are some of the ways that direct positive suggestions were present in the lesson? Indirect positive suggestions?

2. How are the arts integrated into the lesson we observed?

3. How is the infantilization of the students encouraged?

B. Apply what you have understood about Suggestopedia.

1. Most teachers do not have control of the kind of lighting that is present in their classrooms. They also do not have access to special, comfortable chairs for their students. This does not mean that they cannot provide an environment designed to reduce the barriers their students bring with them, however. Can you think of ways that you might do this?

2. Choose a theme, select some music, and plan a visualization exercise. The theme can be about any experience, not necessarily that of taking a trip.

3. Make a list of ten grammatical points about the target language that you would want to display on posters to encourage beginning students' peripheral learning.

EXTRA READING

Lozanov, Georgi. 1982. Suggestology and suggestopedia. In *Innovative approaches to language teaching*, ed. Robert W. Blair. Rowley, Mass.: Newbury House Publishers, Inc.

————. 1978. *Outlines of suggestology and suggestopedy*. London: Gordon and Breach.

O'Connell, Peter. 1982. Suggestopedy and the adult language learner. In *Humanistic approaches: An empirical view*, ELT Documents # 113. London: The British Council.

Racle, Gabriel. 1979. Can suggestopaedia revolutionize language teaching? *Foreign Language Annals* 12:39–40.

Stevick, Earl. 1980. Chapters 18 and 19 in *A way and ways*. Rowley, Mass.: Newbury House Publishers, Inc.

CHAPTER SEVEN

COMMUNITY LANGUAGE LEARNING

INTRODUCTION*

The method we will examine in this chapter advises teachers to consider their students as "whole persons." Whole-person learning means that teachers consider not only their students' feelings and intellect, but also have some understanding of the relationship among students' physical reactions, their instinctive protective reactions and their desire to learn. The Community Language Learning Method takes its principle from the more general Counseling-Learning approach developed by Charles A. Curran. Curran studied adult learning for many years. He discovered that adults often feel threatened by a new learning situation. They are threatened by the change inherent in learning and by the fear that they will appear foolish. Curran believed that a way to deal with the fears of students is for teachers to become "language counselors." A language counselor does not mean someone trained in psychology; it means someone who is a skillful understander of the struggle students face as they attempt to internalize another language. The teacher who can "understand" can indicate his acceptance of the student. By understanding students' fears and being sensitive to them, he can help students overcome their negative feelings and turn them into positive energy to further their learning.

Let us see how Curran's ideas are put into practice in the Com-

---

* In this chapter, the author has benefited enormously from the careful reading and helpful comments of Jennybelle Rardin and Pat Tirone of the Counseling-Learning Institute.

munity Language Learning Method. We will observe a class in a private
language institute in Indonesia. Most of the students work during the
day and come for language instruction in the evening. The class meets
two evenings a week for two hours a session. This is the first class.

EXPERIENCE

The students arrive and take their seats. The chairs are in a circle around
a table that has a tape recorder on it. After greeting the students, the
teacher introduces himself and has the students introduce themselves.
In Indonesian, he tells the students what they will be doing that evening: They are going to have a conversation in English with his help.
The conversation will be tape-recorded, and afterward, they will create
a written form of the conversation—a transcript. He tells the class the
rest of the evening will be spent doing various activities with the
language on the transcript. He then explains how the students are to
have the conversation.

"Whenever one of you would like to say something, raise your
hand and I will come behind you. I will not be a participant in the
conversation except to help you say in English what you want to say.
Say what you want to say in Indonesian; I will give you the English
translation. I will give you the translation in phrases, or 'chunks.' Record
only the chunks, one at a time. After the conversation, when we listen
to the recording, your sentence will sound whole. Only your voices
in English will be on the tape. Since this is your first English conversation, you may want to keep it simple. We have ten minutes for this
activity."

No one speaks at first. Then a young woman raises her hand.
The teacher walks to her chair. He stands behind her. "*Selamat sore,*"
she says. The teacher translates, "Good. . . ." After a little confusion
with the switch on the microphone, she puts "Good" on the tape and
turns the switch off. The teacher then gives "evening," and she tries
to say "evening" in the microphone but only gets out "eve. . . ." The
teacher says again in a clear and warm voice, somewhat exaggerating
the word, "Eve. . .ning." The woman tries again. She shows some
signs of her discomfort with the experience, but she succeeds in putting the whole word "evening" onto the recording.

Another student raises his hand. The teacher walks to him and stands behind his chair. "*Selamat sore*," the second student says to the first student. "*Apa kabar?*" he asks of a third. The teacher, already sensing that this student is a bit more secure, gives the entire translation, "Good evening." "Good evening," the student says, putting the phrase on the tape. "How are you?" the teacher continues. "How . . .," the student says into the microphone, then turns, obviously seeking help for the rest of the phrase. The teacher, realizing he misjudged the student's security, repeats each word separately. "How," repeats the teacher. "How," says the student into the microphone. "Are," repeats the teacher. "Are," the student says. "You," completes the teacher. "You," the student records.

The student to whom the question was directed raises his hand and the teacher stands behind him. "*Kabar baik. Terima kasih,*" he responds. "Fine," the teacher says. "Fine," the student records. "Thank you," the teacher completes. "Thank you," the student securely puts on the tape.

A fourth student asks of another, "*Nama saudara siapa?*" The teacher steps behind her and says, "What's . . . your . . . name?" pausing after each word to give the student time to put her question successfully on the tape.

The other student replies, "*Nama saya Saleh.*" "My name is Saleh," the teacher says in English. "*Apa kabar?*" another student asks Saleh. "How are you?" the teacher translates. "*Saya tidak sehat,*" Saleh answers. "I am not well," the teacher translates. "*Mengapa?*" asks another student. "Why?" says the teacher. "*Sebab kepala saya pusing,*" Saleh replies. "Because I have a headache," translates the teacher. Each of these English utterances is recorded in the manner of the earlier ones, the teacher aware of what size chunk each student can handle. The teacher then announces that they have five minutes left. The conversation continues like this for the five remaining minutes. During this time the students ask each other why they are studying English, what they do for a living, and what their hobbies are. In this conversation, each student around the table records some English utterance on the tape.

After the conversation has ended, the teacher sits in the circle and asks the students in Indonesian how they feel about the experience. One student says that he doesn't remember any of the English he has just heard. The teacher accepts what he says and responds, "You have a concern that you haven't learned any English." The student says, "Yes." Another student says he, too, hasn't learned any English; he was just involved in the conversation. The teacher accepts this comment and replies, "Your attention was on the conversation, not on the English." Another student says that she doesn't mind the fact that she can't remember any English ; she has enjoyed the conversation. The teacher accepts her comment and reassures her and all the students that they will yet have an opportunity to learn the English words— that he does not expect them to remember the English phrases at this time. "Would anyone else like to say anything?" the teacher asks. Since there is silence, the teacher continues, "OK, then. Let's listen to your conversation. I will play the tape. Just listen to your voices in English." The students listen. "OK," the teacher says. "I am going to play the tape again and stop it at the end of each sentence. See if you can recall what you said, and say it again in Indonesian to be sure that everyone understands what was said. If you can't recall your own sentence, we can all help out." They have no trouble recalling what was said.

Next the teacher asks them to move their chairs into a semicircle and to watch as he writes the conversation on the blackboard. The teacher asks if anyone would like to operate the tape recorder and stop it at the end of each sentence. No one volunteers, so the teacher operates it himself. The teacher then writes line by line, numbering each sentence, leaving enough space to write the Indonesian translation under each English sentence. One student asks if he can copy the sentences. The teacher asks him not to at this point and reassures him that there will be time for that later, if not in this class session, then in the next.

The teacher writes all the English sentences. Before going back to put in the Indonesian equivalents, he quietly underlines the first English word and then pauses. Since no one volunteers the meaning, after a few seconds he writes the literal Indonesian translation. He continues this way until all the sentences are translated.

Next, the teacher tells the students to sit back and relax as he reads the transcript of the conversation. He reads it three times. The students just listen.

For the next activity, the "Human Computer[T.M.]," the students are told in a warm manner, "For the next five to ten minutes I am going to turn into a 'human computer' for you. You may use me to practice the pronunciation of any English word or phrase or entire sentence on the transcript. Raise your hand and I'll come behind you. Then you say either the sentence number or the word in English or Indonesian you want to practice. As the computer I am programmed to give back only correct English, so you will have to listen carefully to see if what you say matches what I am saying. You may repeat the word, phrase, or sentence as many times as you want. I will stop only when you stop. You control me; you turn the computer on and off."

A student raises his hand and says, "Thank you." He has trouble with the sound at the beginning of "thank." The teacher models the phrase. The student says it again. The teacher repeats it. Three more times the student starts the computer by saying, "Thank you." After the teacher has said it for the third time, the student stops, which in turn stops the computer.

Another student raises his hand and says, "'What do you do?" a question from the transcript. Again the teacher moves behind the student and repeats the question the student has chosen to practice. The student works on this question several times just as the first student did. Several others practice saying some part of the transcript in a similar manner.

The teacher then asks the students to work in groups of three to create new sentences based upon the words and phrases of the transcript. Each group writes its sentences down. The teacher walks from group to group to help. The first group writes the sentence "Ismael not work in a bank." The teacher repeats the group's sentence correctly, "Ismael does not work in a bank." The second group writes "What is my name?" "OK," says the teacher. After the teacher finishes helping the group, each group reads its sentences to the class.

The teacher replays the tape two times more while the students listen.

Finally, the teacher tells the class they have ten minutes left in the session. He asks them to talk about the experience they have had that evening. As students respond, the teacher understands each student in such a way that each feels he or she has been understood. Most of the students are positive about the experience, one student saying that it is the first time she has felt so comfortable in a beginning language class. "I now think I can learn English," she says.

For the next two classes the students continue to work with the conversation they created. Some of the activities are as follows:

1. The teacher selects the verb "be" from the transcript, and together he and the students conjugate it for person and number in the present tense. They do the same for the verb "do" and for the regular verb "work."

2. The students work in small groups to make sentences with the new forms. They share the sentences they have created with the rest of the class.

3. Students take turns reading the transcript, one student reading the English and another reading the Indonesian. They have an opportunity to work on their English pronunciation again as well.

4. The teacher puts a picture of a person on the blackboard and the students ask questions of that person as if they have just met him.

5. The students reconstruct the conversation they have created.

6. They create a new dialog using words they have learned how to say during their conversation.

When they finish these activities, the class has another conversation, records it, and uses the new transcript as the basis for subsequent activities.

THINKING ABOUT THE EXPERIENCE

Let us now turn our attention to analyzing what we saw. On the left, we can list our observations, and on the right, we can list the principles we derive from our observations.

Observations

1. The teacher greets the students, introduces himself, and has the students introduce themselves.

2. The teacher tells the students what they are going to do that evening. He explains the procedure of the first activity and sets a time limit.

3. Students have a conversation.

4. The teacher stands behind the students.

5. The teacher translates what the students want to say in chunks.

6. The teacher tells them that they have only a few minutes remaining for the conversation.

7. Students are invited to talk about how they felt during the conversation.

Principles

Building a relationship with and among students is very important.

Any new learning experience can be threatening. When students have an idea of what will happen in each activity, they often feel more secure. People learn best when they feel secure.

Language is for communication.

The superior knowledge and power of the teacher can be threatening. If the teacher does not remain in the front of the classroom, the threat is reduced and the students' learning is facilitated. Also this fosters interaction among students, rather than from student to teacher.

The teacher should be sensitive to students' limitations and not overwhelm them with more than they can handle.

Students feel more secure when they know the limits of an activity.

Teacher and students are whole persons.

Observations	**Principles**
8. The teacher accepts what each student says.	Guided by the knowledge that each learner is unique, the teacher creates an accepting atmosphere. Learners feel free to lower their defenses and the learning experience becomes less threatening.
9. The teacher understands what the students say.	The teacher "counsels" the students. He shows them he is really listening to them and understands what they are saying. By understanding how students feel, the teacher can help students to overcome their negative feelings, which might otherwise block their learning.
10. The students listen to the tape and give the Indonesian translation.	The students' native language is used to make the meaning clear. Students feel more secure when they understand everything.
11. The teacher asks the students to form a semicircle in front of the blackboard so they can see easily.	The teacher should take the responsibility for clearly structuring activities in the most appropriate way possible for successful completion of an activity.
12. The teacher reassures the students that they will have time later on to copy the sentences.	Learning at the beginning stages is facilitated if students attend to one task at a time.

Observations	**Principles**
13. Before the teacher puts in the Indonesian equivalents, he pauses. If no one volunteers the meaning, he writes it himself.	The teacher encourages student initiative and independence.
14. The teacher reads the transcript three times. The students relax and listen.	Students need quiet reflection time in order to learn.
15. In the Human Computer^{T.M.} activity, the students choose which phrase they want to practice pronouncing; the teacher, following the student's lead, repeats the phrase until the learner is satisfied and stops.	Students learn best when they have a choice in what they practice. Students develop an inner wisdom about where they need to work. If students feel in control, they can take more responsibility for their own learning.
16. The students have to listen carefully to see if what they say matches what the teacher is saying.	Students need to learn to discriminate; for example, in perceiving the similarities and differences among the target language forms.
17. Students work together in groups of three.	In groups, students can begin to feel a sense of community and can learn from each other as well as the teacher. Cooperation, not competition, is encouraged.
18. The teacher corrects by repeating correctly the sentence the students have created.	Teachers should work in a non-threatening way with what the learner has produced.
19. The students read their sentences to the other members of the class.	Developing a community among the class members builds trust and can help to reduce the threat of the new learning situation.

Observations

Principles

20. The teacher plays the tape while the students listen.

Learning tends not to take place when the material is too new or, conversely, too familiar. Retention will best take place somewhere in between novelty and familiarity.

21. The students are once again invited to talk about the experience they had that evening.

In addition to reflecting on the language, students reflect on what they have experienced. In this way, they have an opportunity to learn about their own learning as well as learning about the language.

22. Other activities with the transcript of the first conversation occur. Then, the learners have a new conversation.

In the beginning stages, the "syllabus" is designed primarily by the students. Students are more willing to learn when they have created the material themselves.

REVIEWING THE PRINCIPLES

Let us now review the principles of the Community Language Learning Method. In answering our ten questions, some additional information about the method will also be provided.

  1. What are the goals of teachers who use the Community Language Learning Method?

Teachers who use the Community Language Learning Method want their students to learn how to use the target language communicatively. In addition, they want their students to learn about their own learning, to take increasing responsibility for it. Both of these are to be accomplished in a nondefensive manner. Nondefensive learning can result when teacher and learner treat each other as a whole person, and do not separate each other's intellect from his or her feelings.

2. What is the role of the teacher? What is the role of the students?

The teacher's initial role is that of a counselor. This does not mean that the teacher is a therapist, or that the teacher does no teaching. Rather, it means that the teacher recognizes how threatening a new learning situation can be for adult learners, so he skillfully understands and supports his students in their struggle to master the target language.

Initially the learner is very dependent upon the teacher. He is a "client" of the counselor's. It is recognized, however, that as the learner continues to study, he becomes increasingly independent. Community Language Learning methodologists have identified five stages in this movement from dependency to independency. During Stage IV, the roles switch. The student no longer needs the teacher's encouragement and absolute sense of security. It is the teacher who needs the understanding and acceptance if he is to continue to give further information. The student knows so much of the language at this point that the teacher is hesitant to correct him. The teacher needs the students to show, in some way, "It's OK to correct me; I'm ready."

3. What are some characteristics of the teaching/learning process?

In a Stage I class, which is what we observed, students typically have a conversation in their native language. The teacher helps them express what they want to say by giving them the target language translation in chunks. These chunks are recorded, and when they are replayed, it sounds like a fairly fluid conversation. Later, a transcript is made of the conversation, and mother tongue equivalents are written beneath the target language words. The transcription of the conversation becomes a "text" with which students work. Various activities are conducted (for example, examination of a grammar point, working on pronunciation of a particular phrase, or creating new sentences with words from the transcript) that allow students to further explore the language they have generated. During the course of the lesson, students are invited to say how they feel, and in return the teacher understands them.

According to Curran, there are six elements necessary for nondefensive learning. The first of these is security. Next is aggression, by which Curran means that students should be given an opportunity to assert themselves, be actively involved, and invest themselves in the learning experience. One way of allowing for this in the lesson we observed was for students to conduct their own conversation. The third element is attention; at a beginning level, students must directly focus on or attend to one task at a time. Recall that the teacher in our lesson asks the students not to copy the transcript while he was writing it on the blackboard. Instead, he wanted them to attend to what he was writing and to add what translation they may have recalled in order to complete the transcript.

The fourth element, reflection, occurred in two different ways in our lesson. The first was when the students reflected on the language as the teacher read the transcript three times. The second was when students were invited to stop and consider the active experience they were having. Retention is the fifth element, the integration of the new material that takes place within your whole self. The last element is discrimination, sorting out the differences among target language forms. We saw this element when the students were asked to listen to the Human Computer$^{T.M.}$ and attempt to match their pronunciation to the computer's.

4. What is the nature of student-teacher interaction? What is the nature of student-student interaction?

The nature of student-teacher interaction in the Community Language Learning Method changes within the lesson and over time. Sometimes the students are aggressive, as when they are having a conversation. At these times, the teacher facilitates their ability to express themselves in the target language. He physically removes himself from the circle, thereby encouraging students to interact with one another. At other times in the lesson, the teacher is very obviously in charge and providing direction. At all times initially, the teacher structures the class; at later stages, the students may assume more responsibility for this. As Rardin has observed, the Community Language Learning Method is neither student-centered, nor teacher-centered, but rather teacher-student centered, with both being decision makers in the class.

Building a relationship with and among students is very important. In a trusting relationship, the threat that students feel is reduced, and therefore, nondefensive learning is promoted. Students can learn from their interaction with each other as well as their interaction with the teacher. A spirit of cooperation, not competition, can prevail.

5. How are the feelings of the students dealt with?

Responding to the students' feelings is considered very important in Counseling-Learning. One regular activity is inviting students to comment on how they feel while the teacher understands. By showing students he understands how they feel, the teacher can help them overcome negative feelings that might otherwise block their learning.

Student security in this lesson was provided for in a number of ways. Some of these were the teacher's use of the students' native language, telling students precisely what they would be doing during the lesson, respecting established time limits, giving students only as much language at a time as they can handle, and taking responsibility for clearly structuring activities in the most appropriate way. While security is a basic element of the learning process, the way in which it is provided will change depending upon which stage the learner is in.

6. How is language viewed? How is culture viewed?

Language is for communication. Curran writes that "learning is persons," that both teacher and student agree to trust one another and the learning process. The focus shifts from grammar and sentence formation to a "sharing and belonging between persons." Curran also believes that language is for developing creative thinking. Culture is integrated with language.

7. What areas of language are emphasized? What language skills are emphasized?

In the early stages, typically the students design the syllabus, in that they decide what they want to be able to say in the target language. Later on the teacher might also work with published textbooks.

Particular grammar points, pronunciation patterns, and vocabulary are worked with, based on the language the students have generated. The most important skills are understanding and speaking the language. Reading and writing are also worked on, however, based upon what the students have already understood.

8. What is the role of the students' native language?

Students' security is initially enhanced by using their native language. Where possible, literal native language equivalents are given to the target language words that have been transcribed. This makes their meaning clear and allows students to combine the target language words in different ways to create new sentences. Directions in class and sessions during which students express their feelings and are understood are conducted in the native language. In later stages, of course, more and more of the target language can be used. Conversations in the target language can, for example, replace native language conversations. In a class where the students speak a variety of native languages, conversations take place right from the start in the target language. Meaning is made clear in other ways, with pantomime, for example.

9. How is evaluation accomplished?

Although no particular mode of evaluation is prescribed in the Community Language Learning Method, whatever evaluation is conducted should be in keeping with the principles of the method. If, for example, the school requires that the students take a test at the end of a course, then the teacher would see to it that the students are adequately prepared for taking it.

Also, a teacher-made classroom test would likely be more of an integrative test than a discrete-point one. Students would be asked to write a paragraph or be given an oral interview, rather than being asked to answer a question which deals with only one point of the language at a time. (Compare this with the evaluation procedures for the Audio-Lingual Method.)

Finally, it is likely that teachers would encourage their students to self-evaluate—to look at their own learning and to become aware of their own progress.

10. How does the teacher respond to student errors?

Teachers should work with what the learner has produced in a nonthreatening way. One way of doing this is for the teacher to repeat correctly what the student has said incorrectly, without calling further attention to the error.

REVIEWING THE TECHNIQUES

We will review the techniques described in this lesson and provide a little more detail. You may have agreed with some or all of the answers to our ten questions and might like to try to incorporate some of these techniques into your own approach to foreign language teaching. Of course, there also may be techniques you are currently using that can be adapted so that they are consistent with the whole-person approach we have explored here.

Tape-recording Student Conversation

This is a technique used to record student-generated language as well as give the opportunity for community learning to come about. By giving students the choice about what to say and when to say it, students are in a good position to take responsibility for their own learning. Students are asked to have a conversation about anything they want, using their mother tongue as the common language of the group (in multi-lingual groups, students' gestures can be used as the common language). After each native language utterance, the teacher translates what the student says into the target language. The teacher gives the students the target language translation in appropriate-sized chunks. Each chunk is recorded, giving students a final tape recording with only the target language on it.

After a conversation has been recorded, it can be replayed. Since the students had a choice in what they wanted to say in the original conversation, it is easier for them to associate meaning with a particular target language utterance. Being able to recall the meaning of almost everything said in a first conversation is motivating for learners. The recording can also be used to simply listen to their voices in the target language.

Recording student conversation works best with twelve or fewer students. In a larger class, students can take turns being the ones to have the conversation.

Transcription

The teacher transcribes the students' tape-recorded target language conversation. Each student is given the opportunity to translate his utterances and the teacher writes the mother tongue equivalent beneath the target language words. Students can copy the transcript after it has been completely written on the blackboard or on large, poster-sized paper, or the teacher may provide them with a copy. The transcript provides a basis for future activities. If poster-sized paper is used, the transcript can be saved and used in a future class for reference.

Reflection on Experience

The teacher takes time during and/or after the various activities to give the students the opportunity to reflect on how they feel about the language learning experience, themselves as learners, and their relationship with one another. As students give their reactions, the teacher understands them—shows that he has listened carefully by giving an appropriate understanding response to what the student has said. He does not repeat what the learner says, but rather shows that he understands its essence. You may wish to return to the lesson we observed where the teacher understood the students' reactions to their conversation. Such responses can encourage students to think about their unique engagement with the language, the activities, the teacher, and the other students, strengthening their independent learning.

Reflective Listening

The students relax and listen to their own voices speaking the target language on the tape. Another possible technique is for the teacher to read the transcript while the students simply listen.

Human Computer[T.M.]

A student chooses some part of the transcript to practice pronouncing. She is "in control" of the teacher when she tries to say the word or phrase. The teacher, following the student's lead, repeats the phrase as often as the student wants to practice it. The teacher does not correct the student's mispronunciation in any way. It is through the teacher's consistent manner of repeating the word or phrase clearly that the student self-corrects as he or she tries to imitate the teacher's model.

Small Group Tasks

The small groups in the class we observed were asked to make new sentences with the words on the transcript. Afterward, the groups shared the sentences they made with the rest of the class. Later in the week, students working in pairs made sentences with the different verb conjugations.

There are a lot of different activities that could occur with students working in small groups. Teachers who use small group activities

believe students can learn from each other and can get more practice
with the target language by working in small groups. Also, small groups
allow students to get to know each other better. This can lead to the
development of a community among class members.

CONCLUSION

As indicated early in this chapter, the particular class that we observed
represents a first class of what is considered a Stage I experience in
the Community Language Learning Method. The principles we have
drawn from it can also be seen in Stage II, III, IV, and V relationships,
although they will be implemented in different ways in order to respond appropriately to learner growth.

The two most basic principles which underlie the kind of learning that can take place in the Community Language Learning Method
are summed up in the following phrases: 1) "Learning is persons,"
which means that both teacher and learner(s) must make a commit-
ment of trust to one another and the learning process; and 2) "Learning is dynamic and creative," which means that learning is a living
and developmental process.

Do you agree with these two basic principles? Do you believe
that a teacher should adopt the role of a counselor, as Curran uses the
term? Should the development of a community be encouraged? Do
you think that students should be given responsibility for, in effect,
creating the syllabus? Which of these or any other principles is compatible with your personal approach to teaching?

Do you think you could use the technique of tape-recording your
students' conversation? Should you give your students an opportunity
to reflect on their experience? Can you use the Human Computer^T.M.?
Which of the other techniques can you see adapting to your teaching
style?

·ACTIVITIES·

A. Check your understanding of the Community Language Learning Method.

1. Curran says there are six elements of effective learning: security, aggression, attention, reflection, retention, and discrimination. Some of the ways these were manifest in our lesson were pointed out in answer to questions 3 and 5. Can you find any other examples of these in the class we observed?

2. Curran claims learners pass through five stages of learning as they go from being a beginning language learner to an advanced language learner. As they pass through these stages, they change from being dependent *on* the teacher to being independent *of* the teacher. Can you see how these students are dependent on the teacher now? Can you find anything in the class we observed that encourages learner independence?

B. Apply what you have understood about the Community Language Learning Method.

1. Have some students tape-record a conversation in their mother tongue. Tell them to record what they wish to learn to say in the language you are teaching. After you have supplied the translation, think of five activities you could use to teach them the target language version while being consistent with the principles of the Community Language Learning Method.

2. Try teaching a lesson as you normally do, but think of your students in a whole-person way if this is a new idea to you. Does this change the way you work? If so, then how?

EXTRA READING

Blair, Robert W., ed. 1982. *Innovative approaches to language teaching.* Rowley, Mass.: Newbury House Publishers, Inc.

Curran, Charles A. 1976. *Counseling-learning in second language.* East Dubuque, Ill.: Counseling-Learning Publications.

————. 1977. *Counseling-learning: A whole-person approach for education.* 2d ed. East Dubuque, Ill.: Counseling-Learning Publications.

Rardin, Jennybelle. 1976. A Counseling-learning model for second language learning. *TESOL Newsletter* X, no. 2 (April).

————. 1982. A humanistic philosophy of education. In *Humanistic approaches: An empirical view*, ELT Document 113. London: The British Council.

————, and Patricia Tirone. 1984. The counseling-learning approach to community language learning. *Proceedings of the 13th annual University of Wisconsin-Milwaukee linguistics symposium.* Milwaukee, Wis.: Department of Linguistics, University of Wisconsin.

Stevick, Earl W. 1980. Chapters 7–17 in *Teaching languages: A way and ways.* Rowley, Mass.: Newbury House Publishers, Inc.

N.B. Other books by Curran and the *C-L/CLL Newsletter* are available from Counseling-Learning Publications, Box 383, East Dubuque, Illinois 61025, U.S.A.

·CHAPTER EIGHT·
THE TOTAL PHYSICAL RESPONSE METHOD

INTRODUCTION

The method we will consider in this chapter is an example of a new general approach to foreign language instruction which has been named "the comprehension approach." It is called this because of the importance it gives to listening comprehension. All the other methods we have looked at have students speaking in the target language from the first day. Methods consistent with the comprehension approach, on the other hand, begin with the listening skill.

The idea of focusing on listening comprehension during early foreign language instruction comes from observing how children acquire their mother tongue. A baby spends many months listening to the people around it long before it ever says a word. The child has the time to try to make sense out of the sounds it hears. No one tells the baby that it must speak. The child chooses to speak when it is ready.

There are several methods being practiced today that have in common an attempt to apply these observations to foreign language instruction. What the methodologists advocate doing during an initial listening period varies from method to method. For example, in Krashen and Terrell's *The Natural Approach* (1983), the students listen to the teacher using the target language communicatively from the beginning of instruction, and communicative activities prevail throughout the course. The teacher helps her students to understand her by using pictures and occasional words in the students' native language and by being as expressive as possible. In many ways the Natural Approach is similar to the Direct Method, which we examined in Chapter Three. One of the ways it is different, however, is that the students are permitted to use their native language along with the target language as they respond to the teacher. This frees them to concentrate on listening comprehension. The teacher does not correct any student errors during oral communication. In Winitz and Reed's self-instructional program and Winitz' *The Learnables*, students listen to tape-recorded words, phrases, and sentences while they look at accompanying pictures. The meaning of the utterance is clear from the context the picture provides. Stories illustrated by pictures are also used as a device to convey abstract meaning. In the Total Physical Response Method, students listen and respond to the spoken target language commands of their teacher.

It is James Asher's Total Physical Response Method we have chosen to examine in detail here in order to see one way in which the principles of the comprehension approach are put into practice. We will learn about these through our usual way of observing a class in which the method is being used. The class is located in Sweden. It is a beginning class for thirty Grade 5 students. They study English for one class period three times a week.

EXPERIENCE*

We follow the teacher as she enters the room and we take a seat in the back of the room. It is the first class of the year so after the teacher takes attendance, she introduces the method they will use to study English. She explains in Swedish, "You will be studying English in a way that is similar to the way you learned Swedish. You will not speak at first. Rather, you will just listen to me and do as I do. I will give you a command to do something in English and you will do the actions along with me. I will need four volunteers to help me with the lesson."

Hands go up and the teacher calls on four students to come to the front of the room and sit with her in chairs that are lined up facing

---

* This lesson is based upon the one in Asher (1982).

the other students. She tells the other students to listen and to watch.

In English the teacher says, "Stand up." As she says it, she stands up and she signals for the four volunteers to rise with her. They all stand up. "Sit down," she says and they all sit. The teacher and the students stand up and sit down together several times according to the teacher's command; the students say nothing. The next time that they stand up together, the teacher issues a new command, "Turn around." The students follow the teacher's example and turn so that they are facing their chairs. "Turn around," the teacher says again and this time they turn to face the other students as before. "Sit down. Stand up. Turn around. Sit down." She says, "Walk," and they all begin walking towards the front row of the students' seats.
"Stop. Jump. Stop. Turn around. Walk. Stop. Jump. Stop. Turn around. Sit down." The teacher gives the commands and they all perform the actions together. The teacher gives these commands again, changing their order and saying them quite quickly. "Stand up. Jump. Sit down. Stand up. Turn around. Jump. Stop. Turn around. Walk. Stop. Turn around. Walk. Jump. Turn around. Sit down."

Once again the teacher gives the commands; this time, however, she remains seated. The four volunteers respond to her commands without her. "Stand up. Sit down. Walk. Stop. Jump. Turn around. Turn around. Walk. Turn around. Sit down." The students respond perfectly. Next, the teacher signals that she would like one of the volunteers to follow her commands alone. One student raises his hand and performs the actions the teacher commands.

Finally, the teacher approaches the other students who have been sitting observing her and their four classmates. "Stand up," she says and the class responds. "Sit down. Stand up. Jump. Stop. Sit down. Stand up. Turn around. Turn around. Jump. Sit down." Even though they have not done the actions before, the students are able to perform according to the teacher's commands.

The teacher is satisfied that the class has mastered these six commands. She begins to introduce some new ones. "Point to the door," she orders. She extends her right arm and right index finger in the direction of the door at the side of the classroom. The volunteers point with her. "Point to the desk." She points to her own big teacher's desk at the front of the room. "Point to the chair." She points to the chair behind her desk and the students follow.

    "Stand up." The students stand up. "Point to the door." The students point. "Walk to the door." They walk together. "Touch the door." The students touch it with her. The teacher continues to command the students as follows: "Point to the desk. Walk to the desk. Touch the desk. Point to the door. Walk to the door. Touch the door.

Point to the chair. Walk to the chair. Touch the chair." She continues
to perform the actions with the students, but changes the order of the
commands. After practicing these new commands with the students
several times, the teacher remains seated and the four volunteers carry
out the commands by themselves. Only once do the students seem confused, at which point the teacher repeats the command which causes
difficulty and performs the action with them.

Next the teacher turns to the rest of the class and gives the following commands to the students sitting in the back row: "Stand up. Sit
down. Stand up. Point to the desk. Point to the door. Walk to the door.
Walk to the chair. Touch the chair. Walk. Stop. Jump. Walk. Turn
around. Sit down." Although she varies the sequence of commands,
the students do not seem to have any trouble following the orders.

Next the teacher turns to the four volunteers and says, "Stand
up. Jump to the desk." The students have never heard this command
before. They hesitate a second and then jump to the desk just as they
have been told. Everyone laughs at this sight. "Touch the desk. Sit
on the desk." Again, the teacher uses a novel command, one they have
not practiced before. The teacher then issues two commands in the
form of a compound sentence, "Point to the door and walk to the door."
Again, the group performs as it has been commanded.

As the last step of the lesson, the teacher writes the new commands on the blackboard. Each time she writes a command, she acts
it out. The students copy the sentences from the blackboard into the
notebooks.

The class is over. No one except the teacher has spoken a word.
However, a few weeks later when we walk by the room we hear a different voice. We stop to listen for a moment. One of the students is
speaking. We hear her say, "Raise your hands. Show me your hands.
Close your eyes. Put your hands behind you. Open your eyes. Shake
hand with your neighbor. Raise your left foot." We look in and see
that the student is directing the other students and the teacher with
these commands. They are not saying anything; they are just following the student's orders.

THINKING ABOUT THE EXPERIENCE

Now that we have observed the Total Physical Response Method being used in a class, let's examine what we have seen. We will list our observations and then try to understand the principles upon which the teacher's behavior is based.

Observations

1. The teacher gives a command in the target language and performs it with the students.

2. The students say nothing.

3. The teacher gives the commands quite quickly.

4. The teacher sits down and issues commands to the volunteers.

5. The teacher directs students other than the volunteers.

Principles

Meaning in the target language can often be conveyed through actions. Memory is activated through learner response. Beginning foreign language instruction should address the right hemisphere of the brain, the part which controls nonverbal behavior. The target language should be presented in chunks, not just word by word.

The students' understanding of the target language should be developed before speaking.

Students can initially learn one part of the language rapidly by moving their bodies.

The imperative is a powerful linguistic device through which the teacher can direct student behavior.

Students can learn through observing actions as well as by performing the actions themselves.

Observations	**Principles**
6. The teacher introduces new commands after she is satisfied that the first six have been mastered.	It is very important that students feel successful. Feelings of success and low anxiety facilitate learning.
7. The teacher changes the order of the commands.	Students should not be made to memorize fixed routines.
8. When the students make an error, the teacher repeats the command while acting it out.	Correction should be carried out in an unobtrusive manner.
9. The teacher gives the students commands they have not heard before.	Students must develop flexibility in understanding novel combinations of target language chunks. They need to understand more than the exact sentences used in training. Novelty is also motivating.
10. The teacher says, "Jump to the desk." Everyone laughs.	Language learning is more effective when it is fun.
11. The teacher writes the new commands on the blackboard.	Spoken language should be emphasized over written language.
12. A few weeks later, a student who hasn't spoken before gives commands.	Students will begin to speak when they are ready.
13. A student says, "Shake hand with your neighbor."	Students are expected to make errors when they first begin speaking. Teachers should be tolerant of them. Work on the fine details of the language should be postponed until students have become somewhat proficient.

REVIEWING THE PRINCIPLES

We will next turn to our ten questions in order to increase our understanding of the Total Physical Response Method.

1. What are the goals of teachers who use the Total Physical Response Method?

Teachers who use the Total Physical Response Method believe in the importance of having their students *enjoy* their experience in learning to communicate in a foreign language. In fact, the Total Physical Response Method was developed in order to reduce the stress people feel when studying foreign languages and thereby encourage students to persist in their study beyond a beginning level of proficiency.

The way to do this, Asher believes, is to base foreign language learning upon the way children learn their native language.

2. What is the role of the teacher? What is the role of the students?

Initially, the teacher is the director of all student behavior. The students are imitators of her nonverbal model. At some point (usually after ten to twenty hours of instruction) some students will be "ready to speak." At that point there will be a role reversal with individual students directing the teacher and the other students.

3. What are some characteristics of the teaching/learning process?

The first phase of a lesson is one of modeling. The instructor issues commands to a few students, then performs the actions with them. In the second phase, these same students demonstrate that they can understand the commands by performing them alone. The observers also have an opportunity to demonstrate their understanding.

The teacher next recombines elements of the commands to have students develop flexibility in understanding unfamiliar utterances. These commands, which students perform, are often humorous.

After learning to respond to some oral commands, the students learn to read and write them. When students are ready to speak, they become the ones who issue the commands. After students begin speaking, activities expand to include skits and games.

4. What is the nature of student-teacher interaction? What is the nature of student-student interaction?

The teacher interacts with the whole group of students and with individual students. Initially the interaction is characterized by the teacher speaking and the students responding nonverbally. Later on, the students become more verbal and the teacher responds nonverbally.

Students perform the actions together. Students can learn by watching each other. At some point, however, Asher believes observers must demonstrate their understanding of the commands in order to retain them.

As students begin to speak, they issue commands to one another as well as to the teacher.

5. How are the feelings of the students dealt with?

One of the main reasons the Total Physical Response Method was developed was to reduce the stress people feel when studying foreign languages. One of the primary ways this is accomplished is to allow learners to speak when they are ready. Forcing them to speak before then will only create anxiety. Also, when students do begin to speak, perfection should not be expected.

Another way to relieve anxiety is to make language learning as enjoyable as possible. The use of zany commands and humorous skits are two ways of showing that language learning can be fun.

Finally, it is important that there not be too much modeling, but that students not to be too rushed either. Feelings of success and low anxiety facilitate learning.

6. How is language viewed? How is culture viewed?

Just as with the acquisition of the native language, the oral modality is primary. Culture is the lifestyle of people who speak the language natively.

7. What areas of language are emphasized? What language skills are emphasized?

Grammatical structures and vocabulary are emphasized over other language areas. These are embedded within imperatives. The imperatives are single words and multi-word chunks. One reason for the use of imperatives is their frequency of occurrence in the speech directed at young children learning their mother tongue.

Understanding the spoken word should precede its production. The spoken language is emphasized over written language. Students often do not learn to read the commands they have already learned to perform until after ten hours of instruction.

8. What is the role of the students' native language?

The method is usually introduced in the students' native language. After the introduction, rarely would the mother tongue be used. Meaning is made clear through body movements.

9. How is evaluation accomplished?

Teachers will know immediately whether or not students understand by observing their students' actions. Formal evaluations can be conducted simply by commanding individual students to perform a series of actions. As students become more advanced, their performance in skits they have created can become the basis for evaluation.

10. How does the teacher respond to student errors?

It is expected that students will make errors when they first begin speaking. Teachers should be tolerant of them and only correct major errors. Even these should be corrected unobtrusively. As students get more advanced, teachers can "fine tune"—correct more minor errors.

REVIEWING THE TECHNIQUES

The major technique, as we saw in the lesson we observed, is the use of commands to direct behavior. Asher acknowledges that, although this technique is powerful, a variety of activities is preferred for maintaining student interest. A detailed description of using commands is provided below. If you find some of the principles of the Total Physical Response Method to be of interest, you may wish to devise your own techniques to supplement this one.

Using Commands to Direct Behavior

It should be clear from the class we observed that the use of commands is the major teaching technique of the Total Physical Response Method. The commands are given to get students to perform an action; the action makes the meaning of the command clear. Since Asher suggests keeping the pace lively, it is necessary for a teacher to plan in advance just which commands she will introduce in a lesson. If the teacher tries to think them up as the lesson progresses, the pace will be too slow.

At first, to clarify meaning, the teacher performs the actions with the students. Later the teacher directs the students alone. The students' actions tell the teacher whether or not the students understand.

As we saw in the lesson we observed, Asher advises teachers to vary the sequence of the commands so that students do not simply memorize the action sequence without ever connecting the actions with the language.

Asher believes it is very important that the students feel successful. Therefore, the teacher should not introduce new commands too fast. It is recommended that a teacher present three commands at a time. After students feel successful with these, three more can be taught.

Although we were only able to observe one beginning class, people always ask just how much of a language can be taught through the use of imperatives. Asher claims that all grammar features can be communicated through imperatives. To give an example of a more advanced lesson, one might teach the past tense as follows:

> TEACHER: Ingrid, walk to the blackboard. (Ingrid gets up and
>   walks to the blackboard.)
> TEACHER: Class, if Ingrid *walked* to the blackboard, stand up.
>   (The class stands up.)
> TEACHER: Ingrid, write your name on the blackboard. (Ingrid
>   writes her name on the blackboard.)
> TEACHER: Class, if Ingrid *wrote* her name on the blackboard,
>   sit down. (The class sits down.)

Role Reversal

Students command their teacher and classmates to perform some actions. Asher says that students will want to speak after ten to twenty hours of instruction, although some students may take longer. Students should not be encouraged to speak until they are ready.

Action Sequence

At one point we saw the teacher give three connected commands. For example, the teacher told the students to point to the door, walk to the door, and touch the door. As the students learn more and more of the target language, a longer series of connected commands can be given, which together comprise a whole procedure. While we did not see a long action sequence in this very first class, a little later on students might receive the following instructions:

Take out a pen.

Take out a piece of paper.

Write a letter. (imaginary)

Fold the letter.

Put it in an envelope.

Seal the envelope.

Write the address on the envelope.

Put a stamp on the envelope.

Mail the letter.

This series of commands is called an action sequence, or an operation. Many everyday activities, like writing a letter, can be broken down into an action sequence that students can be asked to perform.

CONCLUSION

Now that we have had a chance to experience a Total Physical Response class and to examine its principles and techniques, you should try to think about how any of this will be of use to you in your own teaching. The teacher we observed was using the Total Physical Response Method with Grade 5 children; however, this same method has been used with adult learners and younger children as well.

Ask yourself: Does it make any sense to delay the teaching of speaking the target language? Do you believe that students should not be encouraged to speak until they are ready to do so? Should a teacher overlook certain student errors in the beginning? Which, if any, of the other principles do you agree with?

Would you use the imperative to present the grammatical structures and vocabulary of the target language? Do you believe it is possible to teach all grammatical features through the imperative? Do you think that accompanying language with action aids recall? Would you teach reading and writing in the manner described in this lesson? Would you want to adapt any of the techniques of the Total Physical Response Method to your teaching situation? Can you think of any others you would create that would be consistent with the principles presented here?

·ACTIVITIES·

A. Check your understanding of the Total Physical Response Method.

1. Asher believes that foreign language instruction can and should be modeled on mother tongue acquisition. What are some characteristics of his method that are similar to the way children acquire their mother tongue?

2. One of the principles of Total Physical Response is that when student anxiety is low, language learning is enhanced. How does this method lower student anxiety?

B. Apply what you have understood about the Total Physical Response Method.

1. Although the teacher uses imperatives, she does so in a gentle, pleasant way, the way a parent would (usually) do with a child. Her voice, facial expression, and manner are kind. Practice giving the commands in this chapter in this way.

2. A lot of target language structures and vocabulary can be taught through the imperative. Plan part of a Total Physical Response lesson in which the present continuous tense, or another structure in the target language, is introduced.

3. In the action sequence (operation) that we looked at, the teacher had the students pretend to write and mail a letter. Think of five other common activities which could be used as action sequences in the classroom. Make a list of commands for each one.

EXTRA READING

Asher, James. 1982. *Learning another language through actions: The complete teacher's guidebook*, 2d ed. Los Gatos, Calif.: Sky Oaks Productions, Inc.

Blair, Robert W., ed. 1982. *Innovative approaches to language teaching*. Rowley, Mass.: Newbury House Publishers, Inc.

Krashen, Stephen, and Tracy Terrell. 1983. *The natural approach: Language acquisition in the classroom*. Hayward, Calif.: The Alemany Press.

Nelson, Gayle, and Thomas Winters. 1980. *ESL operations*. Rowley, Mass.: Newbury House Publishers, Inc.

Romijn, Elizabeth, and Contee Seely. 1982. *Live action English for foreign students*. San Francisco, Calif.: Alemany Press.

Seely, Contee. 1982. Total physical response is more than commands—At all levels. *Cross-Currents* IX:2, 45–65.

Winitz, Harris. 1978. *The learnables*. Kansas City, Mo.: International Linguistics. Cassette program series.

———, ed. 1981. *The Comprehension approach to foreign language instruction*. Rowley, Mass.: Newbury House Publishers, Inc.

N.B. Total Physical Response films and other materials may be obtained through Sky Oaks Productions, Inc., P.O. Box 1102, Los Gatos, California 95031, U.S.A.

CHAPTER NINE

THE COMMUNICATIVE APPROACH

INTRODUCTION

You may have noticed that originators of most of the methods discussed in this book take as their primary goal enabling students to communicate using the target language. Many of these same methodologists emphasize the acquisition of linguistic structures or vocabulary. Adherents of the Communicative Approach, which we will consider in this chapter, acknowledge that structures and vocabulary are important. However, they feel that preparation for communication will be inadequate if only these are taught. Students may know the rules of language *usage*, but will be unable to *use* the language.

When we communicate, we use the language to accomplish some function, such as arguing, persuading, or promising. Moreover, we carry out these functions within a social context. A speaker will choose a particular way to express his argument not only based upon his intent and his level of emotion, but also on whom he is addressing and what his relationship with that person is. For example, he may be more direct in arguing with his friend than with his employer.

Furthermore, since communication is a process, it is insufficient for students to simply have knowledge of target language forms, meanings, and functions. Students must be able to apply this knowledge in negotiating meaning. It is through the interaction between speaker and listener (or reader and writer) that meaning becomes clear. The listener gives the speaker feedback as to whether or not he understands what the speaker has said. In this way, the speaker can revise what he has said and try to communicate his intended meaning again, if necessary.

Let us see how this notion of communication is put into practice in the Communicative Approach. The class we will visit is one being conducted for immigrants to the United States. These twenty people have lived in the United States for two years and are at a high-intermediate level of English proficiency. They meet two evenings a week for two hours each class.

EXPERIENCE

The teacher greets the class and distributes a handout. There is writing on both sides. On one side is a copy of a sports column from a recent newspaper. The reporter discusses who he thinks will win the World Cup. The teacher asks the students to read it and then to underline the predictions the reporter has made. He gives them these and all other directions in the target language. When the students have finished, they read what they have underlined. The teacher writes the predictions on the blackboard. Then he and the students discuss which predictions the reporter feels more certain about and which predictions he feels less certain about.

> Malaysia is very likely to win the World Cup this year.
> Italy can win if they play as well as they have lately.
> Czechoslovakia probably won't be a contender.
> England may have an outside chance.

Then he asks the students to look at the first sentence and to tell the class another way to express this same prediction. One student says, "Malaysia probably will win the World Cup." "Yes," says the teacher. "Any others?" No one responds. The teacher offers, "Malaysia is almost certain to win the World Cup." "What about the next?" he asks the class. One student replies, "It is possible that Italy will win the World Cup." Another student offers, "There's a possibility that Italy will win the World Cup." Each of the reporter's predictions is discussed in this manner. All the paraphrases the students suggest are evaluated by the teacher and the other students to make sure they convey the same degree of certainty as the reporter's original prediction.

Next, the teacher asks the students to turn to the other side of the handout. On it are all the sentences of the article that they have been working on. They are, however, out of order. For example, the first two sentences on this side of the handout are:

> England may have an outside chance. In the final
> analysis, the winning team may simply be the one with the
> most experience.

The first sentence was in the middle of the original sports column. The second was the last sentence of the original column. The teacher tells the students to unscramble the sentences, to put them in their proper order once again. When they finish, the students compare what they have done with the original on the other side of the handout.

The teacher next announces that the students will be playing a game. He divides the class into small groups containing five people each. He hands each group a deck of thirteen cards. Each card has a picture of a piece of sports equipment. As the students identify the items, the teacher writes each name on the blackboard: basketball, soccer ball, volleyball, tennis racket, skis, ice skates, roller skates, football, baseball bat, golf clubs, bowling ball, badminton racket, and hockey stick.

The cards are shuffled and four of the students in a group are dealt three cards each. They do not show their cards to anyone else. The extra card is placed face down in the middle of the group. The fifth person in each group receives no cards. She is told that she should try to predict what it is that Dumduan (one of the students in the class) will be doing the following weekend. The fifth student is to make statements like, "Dumduan may go skiing this weekend." If one of the members of his group has a card showing skis, the group member would reply, for example, "Dumduan can't go skiing, because I have her skis." If, on the other hand, no one has the picture of the skis, then the fifth student can make a strong statement about the likelihood of Dumduan going skiing. She can say, for example, "Dumduan will go skiing." She can check her prediction by turning over the card that was placed face down. If it is the picture of the skis, then she knows she is correct.

The students seem to really enjoy playing the game. They take turns so that each person has a chance to make the predictions about how a classmate will spend his or her time.

For the next activity, the teacher reads a number of predictions like the following:

In 1992, a woman will be elected President of the
United States.

By 2000, solar energy will replace the world's
reliance on fossil fuels.

By 2050, people will be living on the moon.

The students are told to make statements about how probable they
think the predictions are and why they believe so. They are also asked
how they feel about the prediction. In discussing one of the predictions, a student says he doesn't think that it's *like* that a world govern-
ment will be in place by the twenty-second century. The teacher and
students ignore his error and the discussion continues.

Next, the teacher has the students divide into groups of three.
Since there are twenty students, there are six groups of three students
and one group of two. One member of each group is given a picture
strip story. There are six pictures in a row on a piece of paper, but
no words. The pictures tell a story. The student with the story shows
the first picture to the other members of his group, while covering
the remaining five pictures.

The other students try to predict what they think will happen in the second picture. The first student tells them whether they are correct or not. He then shows them the second picture and asks them to predict what the third picture will look like. After the entire series of pictures has been shown, the group gets a new strip story and they change roles, giving the first student an opportunity to work with a partner in making predictions.

For the final activity of the class, the students are told that they will do a role-play. The teacher tells them that they are to be divided into groups of four. They are to imagine that they are all employees of the same company. One of them is the others' boss. They are having a meeting to discuss what will possibly occur as a result of their company merging with another company. Before they begin, they discuss some possibilities together. They decide that they can talk about topics such as whether or not some of the people in their company will lose their jobs, whether or not they will have to move, whether or not certain policies will change, whether or not they will earn more money. "Remember," reminds the teacher, "that one of you in each group is the boss. You should think about this relationship if, for example, he makes a prediction that you don't agree with."

For fifteen minutes the students perform their role-play. The teacher moves from group to group to answer questions and offer any advice on what the groups can discuss. After it's over, the students have an opportunity to pose any questions. In this way, they elicit some relevant vocabulary words. They then discuss what language forms are appropriate in dealing with one's boss. "For example," the teacher explains, "what if you know that your boss doesn't think that the vacation policy will change, but you think it will. How will you state your prediction? You are more likely to say something like 'I think the vacation policy might change,' than 'The vacation policy will change.' "

"What if, however," the teacher says, "it is your colleague with whom you disagree and you are certain that you are right. How will you express your prediction then?" One student offers, "I know that the vacation policy will change." Another student says, "I am sure that the vacation policy will change." A third student says simply, "The vacation policy will change."

The class is almost over. The teacher uses the last few minutes to give the homework assignment. The students are to listen to the debate between two political candidates on the radio or watch it on television that night. They are then to write their prediction of who they think will win the election and why they think so. They will read these to their classmates at the start of the next class.

THINKING ABOUT THE EXPERIENCE

As we have seen before, there are important principles underlying the behavior we have observed. Let us now investigate these by compiling our two lists of our observations and the underlying principles.

Observations	Principles
1. The teacher distributes a handout that has a copy of a sports column from a recent newspaper.	Whenever possible, "authentic language"—language as it is used in a real context—should be introduced.
2. The teacher tells the students to underline the reporter's predictions and to say which ones they think the reporter feels most certain of and which he feels least certain of.	Being able to figure out the speaker's or writer's intentions is part of being communicatively competent.
3. The teacher gives the students the directions for the activity in the target language.	The target language is a vehicle for classroom communication, not just the object of study.
4. The students try to state the reporter's predictions in different words.	One function can have many different linguistic forms. Since the focus of the course is on real language use, a variety of linguistic forms are presented together.

Observations

5. The students unscramble the sentences of the newspaper article.

Principles

Students should work with language at the discourse or supra-sentential (above the sentence) level. They must learn about cohesion and coherence, those properties of language which bind the sentences together.

6. The students play a language game.

Games are important because they have certain features in common with real communicative events—there is a purpose to the exchange. Also, the speaker receives immediate feedback from the listener on whether or not she has successfully communicated. Having students work in small groups maximizes the amount of communicative practice they receive.

7. The students are asked how they feel about the predictions.

Students should be given an opportunity to express their ideas and opinions.

8. A student makes an error. The teacher and other students ignore it.

Errors are tolerated and seen as a natural outcome of the development of communication skills. Students' success is determined as much by their fluency as it is by their accuracy.

9. The teacher gives each group of students a strip story and a task to perform.

One of the teacher's major responsibilities is to establish situations likely to promote communication.

Observations	**Principles**
10. The students work with a partner to predict what the next picture in the strip story will look like.	Communicative interaction encourages cooperative relationships among students. It gives students an opportunity to work on negotiating meaning.
11. The students are to do a role-play. They are to imagine that they are all employees of the same company.	The social context of the communicative event is essential in giving meaning to the utterances.
12. The teacher reminds the students that one of them is playing the role of the boss and that they should remember this when speaking to her.	Learning to use language forms appropriately is an important part of communicative competence.
13. The teacher moves from group to group offering advice and answering questions.	The teacher acts as an advisor during communicative activities.
14. The students suggest alternative forms they would use to state a prediction to a colleague.	In communicating, a speaker has a choice not only about what to say, but also how to say it.
15. After the role-play is finished, the students elicit relevant vocabulary.	The grammar and vocabulary that the students learn follow from the function, situational context, and the roles of the interlocutors.
16. For their homework, the students are to listen to a debate on the radio or watch it on television.	Students should be given opportunities to develop strategies for interpreting language as it is actually used by native speakers (Littlewood 1981).

REVIEWING THE PRINCIPLES

The answers to our ten questions will help us come to a better under-standing of the Communicative Approach. In some answers new information has been provided to clarify certain concepts.

1. What is the goal of teachers who use the Communicative Approach?

The goal is to have one's students become communicatively competent. While this has been the stated goal of many of the other methods, in the Communicative Approach the notion of what it takes to be communicatively competent is much expanded.

Communicative competence involves being able to use the language appropriate to a given social context. To do this students need knowledge of the linguistic forms, meanings, and functions. They need to know that many different forms can be used to perform a function and also that a single form can often serve a variety of functions. They must be able to choose from among these the most appropriate form, given the social context and the roles of the interlocutors. They must also be able to manage the process of negotiating meaning with their interlocutors.

2. What is the role of the teacher? What is the role of the students?

The teacher is a facilitator of his students' learning. As such he has many roles to fulfill. He is a manager of classroom activities. In this role, one of his major responsibilities is to establish situations likely to promote communication. During the activities he acts as an advisor, answering students' questions and monitoring their performance. At other times he might be a "co-communicator"—engaging in the communicative activity along with the students (Littlewood 1981).

Students are, above all, communicators. They are actively engaged in negotiating meaning—in trying to make themselves understood—even when their knowledge of the target language is incomplete. They learn to communicate by communicating.

Also, since the teacher's role is less dominant than in a teacher-centered method, students are seen as more responsible managers of their own learning.

3. What are some characteristics of the teaching/learning process?

The most obvious characteristic of the Communicative Approach is that almost everything that is done is done with a communicative intent. Students *use* the language a great deal through communicative activities such as games, role-plays, and problem-solving tasks (see discussion of these in the review of techniques).

Activities that are truly communicative, according to Morrow (in Johnson and Morrow 1981), have three features: information gap, choice, and feedback.

An information gap exists when one person in an exchange knows something that the other person doesn't. If we both know today is Tuesday and I ask you, "What is today?" and you answer, "Tuesday," our exchange isn't really communicative.

In communication, the speaker has a choice of what she will say and how she will say it. If the exercise is tightly controlled so that students can only say something in one way, the speaker has no choice and the exchange, therefore, is not communicative. In a chain drill, for example, if a student must reply to her neighbor's question in the same way as her neighbor replied to someone else's question, then she has no choice of form and content, and real communication does not occur.

True communication is purposeful. A speaker can thus evaluate whether or not her purpose has been achieved based upon the information she receives from her listener. If the listener does not have an opportunity to provide the speaker with such feedback, then the exchange is not really communicative. Forming questions through a transformation drill may be a worthwhile activity, but it is not communicative since a speaker will receive no response from a listener. She is thus unable to assess whether her question has been understood or not.

Another characteristic of the Communicative Approach is the use of authentic materials. It is considered desirable to give students an opportunity to develop strategies for understanding language as it is actually used by native speakers.

Finally, we noted that activities in the Communicative Approach are often carried out by students in small groups. Small numbers of students interacting are favored in order to maximize the time allotted to each student for learning to negotiate meaning.

4. What is the nature of student-teacher interaction? What is the nature of student-student interaction?

The teacher is the initiator of the activities, but he does not always himself interact with the students. Sometimes he is a co-communicator, but more often he establishes situations that prompt communication between and among the students.

Students interact a great deal with one another. They do this in various configurations: pairs, triads, small groups, and whole group.

5. How are the feelings of the students dealt with?

One of the basic assumptions of the Communicative Approach is that students will be more motivated to study a foreign language since they will feel they are learning to do something useful with the language they study.

Also, teachers give students an opportunity to express their individuality by having them share their ideas and opinions on a regular basis. This helps students "to integrate the foreign language with their own personality and thus to feel more emotionally secure with it." (Littlewood 1981, 94).

Finally, student security is enhanced by the many opportunities for cooperative interactions with their fellow students and the teacher.

6. How is language viewed? How is culture viewed?

Language is for communication. Linguistic competence, the knowledge of forms and meanings is, however, just one part of communicative competence. Another aspect of communicative competence is knowledge of the functions language is used for. As we have seen in this lesson, a variety of forms can be used to accomplish a single function. A speaker can make a prediction by saying, for example, "It may rain," or "Perhaps it will rain." Conversely, the same form of the language can be used for a variety of functions. "May," for instance, can be used to make a prediction or to give permission ("They may sit in the back") (Celce-Murcia and Larsen-Freeman, 1983).

Thus, the learner needs knowledge of forms and meanings and functions. However, he must also use this knowledge and take into consideration the social situation in order to convey his intended meaning appropriately. A speaker can seek permission using "may" ("May I have a piece of fruit?"); however, if the speaker perceives his listener as being more of a social equal or the situation as being informal, he would more likely use "can" to seek permission ("Can I have a piece of fruit?").

Culture is the everyday lifestyle of people who use the language natively. There are certain aspects of it that are especially important to communication—the use of nonverbal behavior, for example, which would therefore receive greater attention in the Communicative Approach.

7. What areas of language are emphasized? What language skills are emphasized?

Language functions are emphasized over forms. Typically, although not always, a functional syllabus is used. A variety of forms are introduced for each function. Only the simpler forms would be presented at first, but as students get more proficient in the target language, the functions are reintroduced and more complex forms are learned. Thus, for example, in learning to make requests, beginning students might practice "Would you . . . ?" and "Could you . . . ?" Highly proficient students might learn "I wonder if you would mind . . . ?"

Students work with language at the suprasentential or discourse level. They learn about cohesion and coherence. For example, in our lesson the students recognized that the second sentence of the scrambled order was the last sentence of the original sports column because of its introductory adverbial phrase, "In the final analysis. . . ." This adverbial phrase is a cohesive device that binds and orders this sentence to the other sentences. The students also recognized the lack of coherence between the first two sentences of the scrambled order, which did not appear connected in any meaningful way.

Students work on all four skills from the beginning. Just as oral communication is seen to take place through negotiation between speaker and listener, so too is meaning thought to be derived from the written word through an interaction between the reader and the writer. The writer isn't present to receive immediate feedback from the reader, of course, but the reader tries to understand the writer's intentions and the writer writes with the reader's perspective in mind. Meaning does not, therefore, reside exclusively in the text, but rather arises through negotiation between the reader and writer.

8. What is the role of the students' native language?

The students' native language has no particular role in the Communicative Approach. The target language should be used not only during communicative activities, but also, for example, in explaining the activities to the students or in assigning homework. The students learn from these classroom management exchanges, too, and realize that the target language is a vehicle for communication, not just an object to be studied.

9. How is evaluation accomplished?

A teacher evaluates not only his students' accuracy, but also their fluency. The student who has the most control of the structures and vocabulary is not always the best communicator.

A teacher can informally evaluate his students' performance in his role as an advisor or co-communicator. For more formal evaluation, a teacher is likely to use a communicative test (for extensive discussion of communicative tests, see Madsen [1983]). This is an integrative test which has a real communicative function. In order to assess their writing skill, for instance, a teacher might ask his students to write a letter to a friend.

10. How does the teacher respond to student errors?

Errors of form are tolerated and are seen as a natural outcome of the development of communication skills. Students can have limited linguistic knowledge and still be successful communicators.

REVIEWING THE TECHNIQUES AND THE MATERIALS

There may be aspects of the Communicative Approach that you find appealing. This review has been provided in the event you wish to try to use any of the techniques or materials associated with the Communicative Approach.

Authentic Materials
To overcome the typical problem that students can't transfer what they learn in the classroom to the outside world and to expose students to natural language in a variety of situations, adherents of the Communicative Approach advocate the use of authentic language materials.

In this lesson we see that the teacher uses a copy of a genuine newspaper article. He also assigns the students homework, requiring they listen to a live radio or television broadcast.

Of course, the class that we observed was at the high intermediate level of proficiency. For students with lower proficiency in the target language, it may not be possible to use authentic language materials such as these. Simpler authentic materials (for example, the use of a weather forecast when working on predictions), or at least ones that are realistic, are most desirable. It is not so important that the materials be genuine as it is that they be used authentically.

Another possibility for the use of authentic materials with a lower level class is to use realia that do not contain a lot of language, but about which a lot of discussion could be generated. Menus in the target language are an example; timetables are another.

Scrambled Sentences

The students are given a passage (a text) in which the sentences are in a scrambled order. This may be a passage they have worked with or one they haven't seen before. They are told to unscramble the sentences so that the sentences are restored to their original order. This type of exercise teaches students about the cohesion and coherence properties of language. They learn how sentences are bound together at the suprasentential level through formal linguistic devices such as anaphoric pronouns, which make a text cohesive, and semantic propositions, which unify a text and make it coherent.

In addition to written passages, students might also be asked to unscramble the lines of a mixed-up dialog. Or they might be asked to put the pictures of a picture strip story in order and write lines to accompany the pictures.

Language Games

Games are used frequently in the Communicative Approach. The students find them enjoyable, and if they are properly designed, they give students valuable communicative practice. Games that are truly communicative, according to Morrow (in Johnson and Morrow 1981), have the three features of communication: information gap, choice, and feedback.

These three features were manifest in the card game we observed in the following way: An information gap existed because the speaker did not know what her classmate was going to do the following weekend. The speaker had a choice as to what she would predict (which sport) and how she would predict it (which form her prediction would take). The speaker received feedback from the members of her group. If her prediction was incomprehensible, then none of the members of her group would respond. If she got a meaningful response, she could presume her prediction was understood.

Picture Strip Story

Many activities can be done with picture strip stories. We suggested one in our discussion of scrambled sentences.

In the activity we observed, one student in a small group was given a strip story. She showed the first picture of the story to the other members of her group and asked them to predict what the second picture would look like. An information gap existed—the students in the groups did not know what the picture contained. They had a choice as to what their prediction would be and how they would word it. They received feedback, not on the form but on the content of the prediction, by being able to view the picture and compare it with their prediction.

The activity just described is an example of using a problem-solving task as a communicative technique. Problem-solving tasks work well in the Communicative Approach because they usually include the three features of communication. What's more, they can be structured so that students share information or work together to arrive at a solution. This gives students practice in negotiating meaning.

Role-play

We already encountered the use of role-plays as a technique when we looked at Suggestopedia. Role-plays are very important in the Communicative Approach because they give students an opportunity to practice communicating in different social contexts and in different social roles. Role-plays can be set up so that they are very structured (for example, the teacher tells the students who they are and what they should say) or in a less structured way (for example, the teacher tells the students who they are, what the situation is, and what they are talking about, but the students determine what they will say). The latter is more in keeping with the Communicative Approach, of course, because it gives the students more of a choice. Notice that role-plays structured like this also provide information gaps since students cannot be sure (as with most forms of communication) what the other person or people will say (there's a natural unpredictability). Students also receive feedback on whether or not they have effectively communicated.

CONCLUSION

Perhaps the greatest contribution of the Communicative Approach is asking teachers to look closely at what is involved in communication. If teachers intend students to use the target language, then they must truly understand all that being communicatively competent entails.

Do you agree with this expanded view of communicative competence? Is achieving communicative competence a goal for which you should prepare your students? Would you adopt a functional syllabus? Should a variety of language forms be presented at one time? Are there times when you would emphasize fluency over accuracy? Do these or any other principles of the Communicative Approach make sense to you?

Would you ever use language games, problem-solving tasks, or role-plays? Should all your activities include the three features of communication? Should authentic language be used? Are there any other techniques or materials of the Communicative Approach that you would find useful?

·ACTIVITIES·

A. Check your understanding of the Communicative Approach.

1. Explain in your own words Morrow's three features of communication: information gap, choice, and feedback. Choose one of the activities in the lesson we observed and say whether or not these three features are present.

2. Why do we say that communication is a process? What does it mean to negotiate meaning?

3. What does it mean to say that the linguistic forms a speaker uses should be appropriate to social context?

B. Apply what you have understood about the Communicative Approach.

1. If you wanted to introduce your friend Paula to Roger, you might say:

> *Roger*, this is (my friend) *Paula*.
> I would like to meet *Paula*.
> Let me present *Paula* to you.
> *Roger*, meet *Paula*.
> Allow me to introduce *Paula*.

In other words, there are a variety of forms for this one function. Which would you teach to a beginning class, an intermediate class, an advanced class? Why?

List linguistic forms you can use for the function of inviting. Which would you teach to beginners? To intermediates? To an advanced class?

2. Imagine that you are working with your students on the function of requesting information. The authentic material you have selected is a railroad timetable. Design a communicative game or problem-solving task in which the timetable is used to give your students practice in requesting information.

3. Plan a role-play to work on the same function as in Exercise 2.

EXTRA READING

Brumfit, Christopher J., and Keith Johnson, eds. 1979. *The communicative approach to language teaching*. Oxford: Oxford University Press.

Celce-Murcia, Marianne, and Diane Larsen-Freeman. 1983. *The grammar book: An ESL/EFL teacher's course*. Rowley, Mass.: Newbury House Publishers, Inc.

Johnson, Keith, and Keith Morrow, eds. 1981. *Communication in the classroom*. Essex: Longman.

Littlewood, William. 1981. *Communicative language teaching*. Cambridge: Cambridge University Press.

Madsen, Harold S. 1983. *Techniques in testing*. Teaching techniques in English as a second language, edited by Russell N. Campbell and William E. Rutherford. Oxford: Oxford University Press.

Widdowson, Henry G. 1979. *Teaching language as communication*. Oxford: Oxford University Press.

Wilkins, David A. 1976. *Notional syllabuses*. Oxford: Oxford University Press.

·EPILOGUE·

It was stated in the Introduction that there were two purposes for this book. The first was to provide information about eight language teaching methods being practiced today. We suggested that a teacher informed about the available choices would make better decisions about methodology.

The second purpose for this book was to encourage you to examine your own beliefs about teaching and learning, on which you can base your methodological decisions. Being clear about this would put you in a better position from which to consider the ideas associated with the methods in this book.

It may be a useful exercise at this point to reconsider these ideas. A good way to do this would be to read the answers to question 1 in each chapter: What is the goal of teachers who use the method? Then read the answers to each question in sequence, in all of the chapters. As you do this you will be reminded of some very big differences that exist among the methods.

Elbow (1973) says there are two basic games one can use when one is looking for truth and faced with conflicting assertions. One can play the "doubting game" or one can play the "believing game." If you play the doubting game, you try to objectively assess each method while you look for weaknesses in it. If you play the believing game, you take each method one at a time and try to believe in it in order to understand it. You try to imagine yourself the originator or a practitioner of the method and to see things as they do.

We are not advocating here that you play one game or the other exclusively. You can't possibly believe in all of the principles associated with these eight methods because some are in direct contradiction with others. You have to sift through what has been presented and weigh it against the evidence of scientific research and your personal experience. You more than likely won't embrace a method wholly; rather you will extract from it what resounds in you (Larsen-Freeman 1983c).

On the other hand, if you do not allow yourself to first believe, if you do not allow yourself to enter into a method and understand it from the inside out, then you may be too quick to dismiss a method or the principles or techniques which comprise it. Thus, as you conclude your reading of this book, we encourage you to review what you have experienced, to seriously entertain the principles and techniques of each method, and then to hold them up to the filter of your own beliefs, needs, and experiences. It is you, after all, who have to make the connection to your own teaching situation. It is you who have to make the informed choice.

EXTRA READING

Elbow, Peter. 1973. *Writing without teachers*. New York: Oxford University Press.
Larsen-Freeman, Diane. 1983c. Getting the whole picture: Language teaching methodologies. Keynote address. First Annual Summer Conference for Language Teachers, June 24–25, Brattleboro, Vermont.